# A PRACTICAL GUIDE TO PAYING OFF YOUR MORTGAGE EARLY

Owning a property is a dream for many people, and borrowing from banks is often essential to achieve this. However, having a mortgage can cause real anxiety because of the latent fear of losing our home if we cannot keep up with mortgage payments. Traditionally, homeowners repay their debt over 25 years, but high house prices have made it necessary to increase the term up to 40 years to make monthly payments affordable. Spreading the debt over a longer period of time not only means that borrowers have to pay more interest, but they are also exposed to other risks such as potential interest rate rises and changes in personal circumstances affecting their mortgage eligibility. These can lead to financial worries, financial stress, and reduced well-being. There are few practical guides available to show borrowers how to manage their mortgage debt more effectively, and how to repay their mortgage quickly so that they are debt-free.

This book seeks to empower consumers, young and old, by providing a roadmap to help borrowers achieve financial security through planning for the future, insuring their income, and setting up an emergency fund. It also outlines simple strategies for an early repayment of debt, including paying off the capital, making extra payments, and monitoring their mortgage debt. In doing so, it aims to help readers improve their general well-being, enhance their financial security, reduce their financial worries, and eliminate their 'mortgage insomnia'.

**Lien Luu** is an associate professor at Coventry Business School, and a qualified financial planner, mortgage adviser, and property investor.

**Sukanlaya Sawang** is a full professor and behavioural scientist at Edinburgh Napier University, where she channels her expertise towards the field of innovation and entrepreneurship.

# A PRACTICAL GUIDE TO PAYING OFF YOUR MORTGAGE EARLY

LIEN LUU AND SUKANLAYA SAWANG

Routledge
Taylor & Francis Group

LONDON AND NEW YORK

Designed cover image: gan chaonan/Getty Images

First published 2025
by Routledge
4 Park Square, Milton Park, Abingdon, Oxon OX14 4RN

and by Routledge
605 Third Avenue, New York, NY 10158

*Routledge is an imprint of the Taylor & Francis Group, an informa business*

*British Library Cataloguing-in-Publication Data*
A catalogue record for this book is available from the British Library

*Library of Congress Cataloging-in-Publication Data*
Names: Luu, Liên, 1967– author. | Sawang, Sukanlaya, author.
Title: A practical guide to paying off your mortgage early / Lien Luu and Sukanlaya
    Sawang.
Description: Abingdon, Oxon ; New York, NY : Routledge, 2025. | Includes
    bibliographical references and index.
Identifiers: LCCN 2024020810 (print) | LCCN 2024020811 (ebook) | ISBN
    9781032286310 (hbk) | ISBN 9781032286303 (pbk) | ISBN 9781003297765 (ebk)
Subjects: LCSH: Mortgage loans. | Finance, Personal.
Classification: LCC HG2040.15 .L88 2025 (print) | LCC HG2040.15 (ebook) |
    DDC 332.7/22—dc23/eng/20240719
LC record available at https://lccn.loc.gov/2024020810
LC ebook record available at https://lccn.loc.gov/2024020811

ISBN: 978-1-032-28631-0 (hbk)
ISBN: 978-1-032-28630-3 (pbk)
ISBN: 978-1-003-29776-5 (ebk)

DOI: 10.4324/9781003297765

Typeset in ITC Galliard
by Apex CoVantage, LLC

# CONTENTS

*List of figures*                                                                    *ix*

*List of tables*                                                                     *xi*

*About the authors*                                                                  *xiii*

*Acknowledgements*                                                                   *xv*

Chapter One    Introduction                                                          1
               References                                                            4

Chapter Two    Introducing the mortgage dilemma:
               unravelling the complexities of homeownership                         7
               2.1. Introduction                                                     7
               2.2. Benefits of homeownership                                        8
               2.3. Homeownership across the globe                                   9
               2.4. Value of global real estate                                      10
               2.5. Personal and household debts                                     11
               2.6. Mortgage and financial stress                                    17
               2.7. Mortgage insomnia and psychological
                    well-being                                                       19
               2.8. Conclusion                                                       21
               References                                                            21

Chapter Three  Weighing the decision: paying off your
mortgage – advantages and disadvantages  27
    3.1. Introduction  27
    3.2. Advantages of paying off your mortgage  27
    3.3. Disadvantages of paying off your mortgage
        early  39
    3.4. Evaluating the choice between repayment
        or overpayment  43
    3.5. Conclusion  44
    References  45

Chapter Four  Mastering money management skills to
accelerate mortgage repayment and achieve
financial freedom  49
    4.1. Introduction  49
    4.2. The single- and two-pronged approaches:
        the early mortgage payoff money
        management strategies  49
    4.3. Personal financial plan  53
    4.4. Prepare a net worth statement  57
    4.5. Prepare an income and expenditure
        statement  58
    4.6. Prepare a budget  61
    4.7. Keep records of spending and saving  63
    4.8. Review your plan  64
    4.9. Apps to help with money management  64
    4.10. Conclusion  66

Chapter Five  Optimising mortgage management strategies  67
    5.1. Introduction  67
    5.2. Affordable mortgage  67
    5.3. Ways to repay a mortgage  68
    5.4. Choice of mortgage  70
    5.5. Save product fees  75
    5.6. Switch to a cheaper deal  75
    5.7. How to pay off a mortgage quickly?  76
    5.8. Extra tactics to accelerate your mortgage
        repayment  78
    5.9. Conclusion  82
    References  83

| | | |
|---|---|---|
| Chapter Six | Shield your wealth: mastering asset protection strategies | 85 |
| | 6.1. Introduction | 85 |
| | 6.2. Unlocking mortgage success: influential factors and risk-reduction techniques | 86 |
| | 6.3. Life's uncertainties: balancing mortgages and the risk of premature death | 87 |
| | 6.4. Types of life insurance | 90 |
| | 6.5. Defending your family's well-being and mortgage from health hazards | 91 |
| | 6.6. Mortgage payment protection insurance | 95 |
| | 6.7. Culture of low savings in UK | 95 |
| | 6.8. Inadequate and complex welfare benefits | 96 |
| | 6.9. Protecting your property | 97 |
| | 6.10. Conclusion | 98 |
| | References | 98 |
| Chapter Seven | Utilising investments for mortgage repayment | 101 |
| | 7.1. Introduction | 101 |
| | 7.2. Background | 101 |
| | 7.3. How to invest and repay mortgage early | 102 |
| | 7.4. General considerations | 106 |
| | 7.5. Specific factors | 107 |
| | 7.6. Why fees matter in investing | 109 |
| | 7.7. Approaches to investing | 109 |
| | 7.8. Individual savings accounts (ISAs) | 110 |
| | 7.9. Conclusion | 111 |
| | References | 111 |
| Chapter Eight | Deciding between paying off mortgage and boosting pension savings | 113 |
| | 8.1. Introduction | 113 |
| | 8.2. Importance of retirement planning | 114 |
| | 8.3. How much income is required in retirement? | 116 |
| | 8.4. Why private savings are necessary? | 118 |
| | 8.5. How much do individuals need to save per month? | 119 |
| | 8.6. Benefits of saving in a pension fund | 120 |

| | 8.7. Pension plans with most flexibility | 121 |
|---|---|---|
| | 8.8. Trade-off between overpaying a mortgage and topping up a pension | 122 |
| | 8.9. Case studies | 125 |
| | 8.10. Conclusion | 127 |
| | References | 128 |
| Chapter Nine | Developing a successful property portfolio | 131 |
| | 9.1. Introduction | 131 |
| | 9.2. Buy-to-let properties in the UK | 132 |
| | 9.3. Why do some people prefer buy-to-let properties as investments? | 133 |
| | 9.4. Raising capital | 142 |
| | 9.5. Strategies with minimal risks | 144 |
| | 9.6. Other ways to make money from property | 149 |
| | 9.7. Conclusion | 150 |
| | References | 150 |
| Chapter Ten | Successful property ownership: the final consideration | 155 |
| | 10.1. Introduction | 155 |
| | 10.2. Purchasing the ideal property type | 155 |
| | 10.3. Mortgage security | 158 |
| | 10.4. Key actions to pay off a mortgage | 159 |
| | 10.5. Leveraging mobile apps to assist with mortgage repayment management | 161 |
| | 10.6. The art of handling your money wisely | 161 |
| | 10.7. Conclusion | 162 |
| | References | 163 |
| Index | | 165 |

# Figures

| | | |
|---|---|---|
| 1.1 | Mortgage debt as % of GDP | 2 |
| 2.1 | Homeownership and renting worldwide | 10 |
| 2.2 | Global value of different assets | 11 |
| 2.3 | Housing tenure by age | 14 |
| 2.4 | Different types of financial stress | 18 |
| 2.5 | Stress-sleep cycle | 20 |
| 3.1 | Length of mortgage and interest | 29 |
| 3.2 | Average annual housing costs, 2020–2022 | 32 |
| 3.3 | Housing wealth equity | 34 |
| 3.4 | Mortgage debt, life insurance and impact on survivors | 37 |
| 3.5 | Dimensions of well-being | 39 |
| 3.6 | How an offset saving account works to reduce the mortgage chargeable balance | 42 |
| 6.1 | Perception of biggest assets in financial value | 87 |
| 6.2 | Rankings of insurance | 93 |
| 8.1 | Income requirements in retirement | 117 |
| 8.2 | State pension inadequate to pay for costs of living | 119 |
| 8.3 | Importance of saving early | 120 |
| 10.1 | Successful property ownership roadmap | 160 |

# Figures

# TABLES

| | | |
|---|---|---|
| 2.1 | Property values, mortgage debt, and loan-to-value ratio | 12 |
| 3.1 | Interest payments at different mortgage terms | 29 |
| 3.2 | Mortgage and inflation | 43 |
| 4.1 | How to prepare a net worth statement | 59 |
| 4.2 | How to prepare an income and expenditure statement | 60 |
| 4.3 | How to prepare a budget | 62 |
| 5.1 | Pros and cons of various mortgage options | 74 |
| 5.2 | Growing popularity of longer-term mortgages | 77 |
| 5.3 | Comparing mortgage deals with fee and no fee | 81 |
| 7.1 | Mortgage interest rates and income tax rates | 108 |
| 7.2 | Investment fees and their impact on overall returns | 109 |
| 7.3 | Types of taxes | 110 |
| 8.1 | Pension and tax relief | 121 |
| 8.2 | Saving early and compound interest | 122 |
| 8.3 | Net cost of pension contributions and tax rates | 123 |
| 8.4 | Value of pension contributions over different investment terms | 124 |
| 8.5 | Pension contribution and tax savings for a 45% taxpayer | 126 |
| 9.1 | Growth of property prices based on 5% increase | 134 |
| 9.2 | Average gross rental income of landlords in the UK | 135 |
| 9.3 | Effects of leverage | 136 |
| 9.4 | Changes in treatment of mortgage interest | 138 |
| 10.1 | Percentage of overpayment and the length of time to repay mortgage | 161 |

# About the Authors

**Lien Luu**  Lien is an associate professor at Coventry Business School, and a qualified financial planner, mortgage adviser, and property investor. Lien bought her first home in London and became an accidental landlord when she moved to Switzerland a year later. After returning to the UK, she worked as a financial planner and a mortgage adviser for more than ten years and specialised in advising clients with building a property portfolio.

She manages her property portfolio and has been active in financial planning, mortgages, and property over the past 25 years. Her passion is to help individuals and young people to buy their first home. She wrote *Buying Your Home: A Practical Guide for First-Time Buyers* with her husband in 2022. This book is a sequel, designed to help individuals make an optimal use of a mortgage and eliminate the biggest debt from their life as soon as possible.

**Sukanlaya Sawang**  Sukanlaya is a full professor and behavioural scientist at Edinburgh Napier University, where she channels her expertise towards the field of innovation and entrepreneurship. Her research primarily focuses on utilising innovative strategies and entrepreneurial principles to enhance health and well-being. Passionate about fostering resilience in both financial and mental aspects, she offers her support to startups and small to medium enterprises (SMEs), helping them thrive in their respective industries.

Sukanlaya embarked on her property journey in Australia, where she purchased her first home. This was followed by acquisitions in England and Scotland, giving her a rich and diverse experience in dealing with mortgages across different regions. These experiences ignited a passion within her: to help homeowners navigate the often-stressful process of securing a mortgage. Her mission is to alleviate 'mortgage insomnia' and help people avoid the detrimental effects that mortgage stress can have on their life and overall well-being.

# ACKNOWLEDGEMENTS

We have received a lot of help and support with the publication of this book.

Kristina Abbotts, our commissioning editor, played a pivotal role in the publication of the book, and her encouragement, support, and enthusiasm allowed us to turn an idea into a book. We are incredibly lucky to have an opportunity to work with her and her team.

Christiana Mandizha, the editorial assistant, has done a brilliant job preparing the manuscript for publication, and is always there ready to help.

Dan Atkinson, Head of Technical at Paradigm Norton, meticulously read through the draft, and his feedback has enhanced the final manuscript immensely.

Ron Wheatcroft, technical manager and vice president at Swiss Re, gave valuable feedback on the protection chapter, and we are very grateful for his comments.

We are also grateful to Dr Baseerit Nissah, Senior Lecturer at the Open University, for all the stimulating discussions.

We would like to thank the editorial board, the anonymous reviewers, and the production team for their invaluable support.

We have enjoyed writing this book and hope you'll like it!

# Chapter One
# Introduction

Owning a property is a dream for many people because it provides us with housing security, gives us the freedom to adapt the property to meet our lifestyle and taste, offers a potential increase in housing wealth, and confers a sense of control and freedom.

Getting a loan or a mortgage from banks is pivotal for many individuals in western countries to achieve their dream due to significant financial resources needed to buy a property. Mortgages have become a social norm in many countries, as they are an essential tool in homeownership and accumulation of housing wealth. However, unaffordable mortgage debt represents a big risk, as unexpected life events can exert a great financial strain on those with an unmanageable level.

Housing debt has reached a high level globally, as can be seen in Figure 1.1. Measured as a percentage of GDP, Australians own the largest amount of mortgage debt – $2.15 trillion Australian dollars (US$1.4 trillion) on 6 million homes in 2022, representing 90% of its GDP (Marshall, 2023). The UK ranks second, with a total mortgage debt of approximately £1.7 trillion (US$2.17 trillion) on 13 million outstanding mortgages (with 8.5 million owner-occupier mortgages) in March 2023, equivalent to 69% of its GDP (Boyle, 2023). USA follows next, with $12.44 trillion of mortgage debt on 83.4 million mortgages, representing 52% of its GDP (Federal Reserve Bank of New York, 2024; Channel, 2023). In comparison, China has a lower level of mortgage

DOI: 10.4324/9781003297765-1

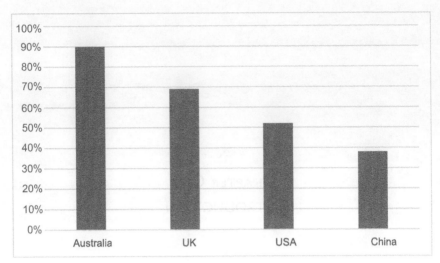

**Figure 1.1** *Mortgage debt as % of GDP*
*Sources:* Marshall, 2023 (Australia); Boyle, 2023 (UK); Federal Reserve Bank of New York, 2024 & Channel, 2023 (US); Servando, 2022 and Palmer, 2022 (China)

debt, at 46 trillion yuan (US$6.8 trillion) in July 2022, representing 38% of its GDP. Mortgages are not as common in China as in the West, as homeowners use their savings or borrow from their extended family, and so only 18% of homeowners are reported to have a mortgage (Servando, 2022; and Palmer, 2022).

The scale and prevalence of mortgage debt is a cause of concern because it affects financial well-being of mortgage holders and their families for several reasons. *Firstly*, mortgage debt is linked to lower financial well-being and greater financial insecurity, causing psychological stress and affecting overall health and quality of life, because it is believed that people are naturally risk-averse and do not like debt (Oussedik et al., 2017).

Mortgage debt in particular causes financial stress because of the fear that inability to pay monthly payments could result in losing one's home. Mortgage contracts represent a long-term financial commitment, normally over 25 years or more, and it is taken as an unwritten assumption that the person will have stable employment and income over this period, which, for most people, will require good health. However, income for some people may not be stable, because their health may deteriorate as they get older, and their employment may not be secure due to the growth of the gig economy, increase in self-employment, as well as changes in the economy. Research shows that employment has been becoming increasingly insecure, with more than half of the workforce in the UK suffering from job insecurity, and nearly a fifth from severe job insecurity (Florisson, 2022, p. 6). Unknown state of health over the long term, and insecure employment resulting in unstable income, can therefore produce real anxiety because mortgages are secured debts, and inability to pay monthly mortgage commitments can result in a loss of home and homelessness.

*Secondly*, the length of mortgage contracts has increased due to high property prices. While mortgages were traditionally repaid over 25 years, it's now common to see repayment terms exceeding 30 years. Some lenders even offer 40-year mortgages, and there were plans for 50-year mortgages. This longer repayment period results in more interest paid. The high cost of housing also means that people are buying homes later, with the average first-time homebuyer now being 34 years old. As a result, mortgages are not just a financial commitment during working years but can extend into retirement.

*Thirdly*, despite the importance of mortgage payments in a household's budget, many families have a limited knowledge of mortgages, and this causes confusion, money worries, and unnecessary high mortgage payments. For example, it is reported that 20% of borrowers in the UK have a variable rate mortgage, which typically costs more than other types. The proportion of homeowners on a variable rate mortgage is higher among more vulnerable groups, such as older and lower-income households. This potentially exposes them to the risk of rising costs when interest rates increase and unaffordability when mortgage payments begin to absorb a larger share of their income. Knowledge can empower individuals to make a better decision regarding mortgages.

*Lastly*, a high level of mortgage debt can affect the stability of the financial system and the wider economy in two ways (Maclennan et al., 2023; Bowe, 2022). The first is the impact on the economy when highly indebted households cut spending drastically, in response to a fall in income, a rise in costs of living and/or a mortgage rate increase, or a decline in perceived wealth (due to falling property prices). Household spending contributes around two-thirds of GDP growth in the UK, and a fall in household spending can exacerbate an economic downturn, increasing levels of unemployment and reducing economic confidence, which in turn can precipitate declining house prices and dwindling housing wealth. Falling house prices make people feel poor through the wealth effect and can further discourage household spending, which in turn affects the wider economy.

The second way mortgage debt can affect the stability of the financial system is the impact of financial losses on lenders. When households face difficulties or are unable to meet their mortgage commitments, this can result in financial losses by banks and lenders. These losses in turn can prompt lenders to become tougher in their lending, reduce credit availability to consumers, businesses, and the wider economy, or, in severe cases, cause banks to collapse. During the Great Financial Crisis of 2007–2009, for example, some governments intervened to stabilise the financial system, in some cases at a great cost. The Irish government spent nearly €46 billion, or 40% of the country's GDP, to bail out Irish banks. The US government is estimated to have spent nearly US$500 billion, or 3.5% of GDP, in 2009 to bail out troubled banks. The UK government injected £137 billion of public money in the form of loans and capital to stabilise the banking sector. Most of the money has been recouped, but £23 billion remained outstanding at the end of January 2018 (Mor, 2018, p. 3; Lucas, 2019). Households' mortgage payments difficulties can spread throughout the financial system and affect the economy, the banking system, individuals, and families.

Knowledge about mortgages or mortgage literacy is therefore crucial as it lays the foundation of financial stability in the economy and the household. This book aims to provide a comprehensive understanding of mortgages, analyse the advantages of early repayment, and outline strategies to accomplish this goal. By the end of this book, readers should feel empowered to actively manage their mortgage and plan for early repayment, resulting in increased enjoyment of their property and greater financial security for themselves and their families. By increasing their own ability to withstand any challenges, households can enhance the financial stability of the housing market, the financial system, and the wider economy.

## References

Bowe, C. (2022). Household indebtedness and financial stability. Available at: www.bankofengland.co.uk/speech/2022/september/colette-bowe-speech-at-the-2nd-research-workshop#:~:text=Household%20indebtedness%20and%20financial%20stability%20%E2%88%92%20speech%20by%20Colette%20Bowe,-Given%20at%20The&text=Colette%20Bowe%20provides%20an%20overview,it%20relates%20to%20financial%20stability [Accessed 6 October 2023].

Boyle, M. (2023). Mortgage statistics: The average UK mortgage size, payments and debt. Available at: www.finder.com/uk/mortgage-statistics [Accessed 12 July 2023].

Channel, J. (2023). Mortgage statistics: 2023. *Lending Tree*. Available at: www.lendingtree.com/home/mortgage/u-s-mortgage-market-statistics/ [Accessed 12 July 2023].

Federal Reserve Bank of New York (2024). Household debt rose by $184 billion in Q1 2024. Available at: https://www.newyorkfed.org/newsevents/news/research/2024/20240514 [Accessed 15 June 2024].

Florisson, R. (2022). The UK insecure work index: Two decades of insecurity. Available at: www.lancaster.ac.uk/media/lancaster-university/content-assets/documents/lums/work-foundation/UKInsecureWorkIndex.pdf [Accessed 12 July 2023].

Lucas, D. (2019). Measuring the cost of bailouts. Available at: http://mitsloan.mit.edu/shared/ods/documents?PublicationDocumentID=7433 [Accessed 6 October 2023].

Maclennan, D., Leishman, C., and Goel, S. (2023). How does the housing market affect financial and economic stability? *Economics Observatory*. Available at: www.economicsobservatory.com/how-does-the-housing-market-affect-financial-and-economic-stability [Accessed 6 October 2023].

Marshall, P. (2023). Australian home loan statistics. Available at: https://mozo.com.au/home-loan-statistics [Accessed 12 May 2023].

Mor, F. (2018). Bank rescues of 2007–09: Outcomes and cost. House of Commons Library Briefing Paper No. 57481. Available at: https://researchbriefings.files.parliament.uk/documents/SN05748/SN05748.pdf [Accessed 6 October 2023].

Oussedik, E., Anderson, M. S., and Feldman, S. R. (2017). Risk versus benefit or risk versus risk: Risk aversion in the medical decision making process. *Journal of Dermatological Treatment*, 28 (1). Available at: www.tandfonline.com/doi/full/10.1080/09546634.2017.1290575 [Accessed 12 July 2023].

Palmer, J. (2022). Chinese mortgage boycott gains steam. *Foreign Policy*. Available at: https://foreignpolicy.com/2022/07/20/china-mortgage-boycott-real-estate-crisis/ [Accessed 12 July 2023].

Servando, K. (2022). Why are people across China refusing to pay their mortgages? What to know so far. Available at: www.bloomberg.com/news/storythreads/2022-07-15/why-are-people-across-china-refusing-to-pay-their-mortgages-what-to-know-so-far [Accessed 12 July 2023].

## Chapter Two
## Introducing the mortgage dilemma
### Unravelling the complexities of homeownership

### 2.1. Introduction

Many of us dream of being mortgage free. This is an important milestone because it ends our mortgage obligations and gives us the financial freedom we yearn for. It marks the beginning of a new stage of life because we now have more money for personal spending, travelling, and enjoying life. Without financial pressures, some of us can afford to work less, take on a less stressful job, or follow our dream of setting up our own business. It is unsurprising that being mortgage free is often synonymous with financial freedom.

Fully paying off our mortgage can also give us more control over our lives and reduce our financial worries. Once a mortgage has been paid off, our lender no longer has a stake in our property. We now have complete ownership and control, and this gives us housing security because we no longer feel worried about losing our home if we cannot afford our mortgage payments. Indeed, paying off a mortgage is a source of pride and represents a sense of achievement because a mortgage is often our biggest debt in life, and repaying it requires careful planning, great determination, financial discipline, and sustained efforts. In the upcoming sections, we will uncover essential tips and tactics for paying off your mortgage faster. But first, let's take a moment to understand the

DOI: 10.4324/9781003297765-2

importance of homeownership, the role of a mortgage, and why it can be one of the most significant financial concerns in our lives.

## 2.2. Benefits of homeownership

Many people around the globe aspire to own their own home. Homeownership is popular because it satisfies a wide range of physical, emotional, and financial needs. Property provides a roof over our head and satisfies our physiological need for shelter and housing. It also meets our need for emotional and ontological security because it gives us a safe haven and a physical and permanent location in the world (Nettleton and Burrows, 1998, pp. 747–748). Living in the same place for a long time allows us to build up a greater sense of belonging and to form better support networks, known as social capital. Owning a home symbolises our financial independence and gives us a sense of pride, social status, and a sense of achievement.

On top of these, there are also good economic justifications for owning a property. In the UK, the leading reasons for buying a home among first-time buyers include a desire to have a sense of control and security, lower cost than renting, and perception of property as a smart investment (Santander, 2019, p. 10). Indeed, it has been shown that owning rather than renting in the UK increases our wealth by £326,000 over 30 years – £200,000 comes from appreciation in the value of the property, and £117,000 savings from monthly spending due to a lower cost of housing (Equity Release Council, 2021, p. 32). In addition, other housing options are increasingly seen to be unviable, as some rental properties are poor quality, insecure, and expensive, while social housing is sold off and not replaced (New Economics Foundation, 2015).

In China, the popularity of homeownership results from a strong desire for ownership, limited available investment opportunities, perceived investment security, and social status and prestige. Homeownership is also a prerequisite for marriage prospects. Due to the one-child policy, China has a large population imbalance, with nearly 34 million more men than women. This means that there is a fierce competition in the marriage market, and a Chinese man is expected to own at least one property before the start of his search for a wife. Over 60% of women in China's major cities believe that a house is necessary before marriage (Juwai, 2017).

In India, a bank highlights nine reasons why owning a home is better than renting, including no landlord issues, emotional security, no uncertainty over a future place to live, no compromise with property requirements, building wealth, tax benefits, easy finance, home as an investment, and social status, as wealth and status are measured by home-ownership (HDFC, 2023).

Homeownership is also good for our health in several ways. First, homeownership improves health through better housing conditions as homeowners tend to invest in their homes. Second, it increases psycho-logical health by providing people with a sense of physical and emotional security, control over their life and safety, and social capital through increased participation in church and community. Third, homeowner-ship is found to increase health through the wealth effect, and the like-lihood of private medical coverage. Indeed, in a study on the impact of the Right to Buy Scheme in the UK, Munford et al. (2020) found that homeownership enhances health via the labour markets with new job opportunities, and that those who go onto become owners are less likely to have unhealthy behaviours (such as smoking), less likely to suf-fer from cardiovascular and respiratory conditions, and more likely to buy health insurance and make fewer visits to their GP. However, they recognise that homeownership could also have a detrimental effect on health if homeowners become anxious about keeping up with mortgage payments (Munford et al., 2020).

## 2.3. Homeownership across the globe

The percentage of homeownership varies greatly around the world, see Figure 2.1. Eastern European countries appear to have the highest level of homeownership. Romania stands at the top, with 95% of its popula-tion owning the home they live in in 2022, followed by Slovakia at 92%, Croatia at 91%, and Lithuania at 88% (Eurostat, 2023). In Romania, homeownership is high because the baby boomers were able to buy the flat they were living in at an affordable price (as cheap as a television) from the government after the fall of communism in 1989. The govern-ment also built few public housing units after 1996, and so private prop-erty became a more popular option by default. The younger generations in Romania also have a high desire to own their own home, due to a lack of viable housing alternatives. The rental market is not well developed and offers poor quality housing and a lack of legal protection for renters. This also applies to other East European countries such as Hungary, Poland, the Czech Republic and Slovakia, Latvia, Lithuania, Bulgaria

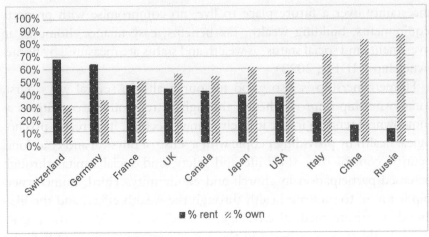

**Figure 2.1** *Homeownership and renting worldwide*
*Source:* WEF (2021)

and Croatia, where there is an absence of a well-developed rental market and where, historically, inhabitants of these countries tended to buy the flat they lived in after the fall of communism (Moldovan, 2018).

China is also a country of homeowners with more than 90% of households owning homes (87% in urban and 96% in rural China). At the same time, more than 20% of Chinese households own multiple homes, higher than many developed countries (Huang et al., 2021).

In contrast, the rate of homeownership is lower in well-developed economies, partly due to higher costs of property, the existence of a well-developed rental market, and stable rents. A survey carried out by the World Economic Forum (2021) shows that renters outnumber homeowners in Switzerland (68% renters v 31% owners) and Germany (64% renters v 35% owners). The split is equal in France, but in the UK and the USA, homeowners outnumber renters.

## 2.4. Value of global real estate

The appeal of property means that global wealth is deeply connected with the housing market. In 2022, the value of all global property reached US$379.7 trillion, with residential property accounting for 76%. As Figure 2.2 shows, the value of property surpasses the combined value of global equities and debt securities and dwarfs the size of global GDP

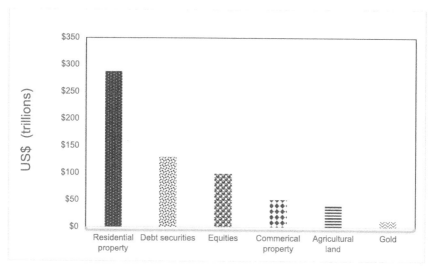

**Figure 2.2** *Global value of different assets*
*Source:* Savills, 2023

($100 trillion). Gold, long used as a store of wealth, also pales in comparison, with the value of all gold ever mined standing at $12 trillion, or 3% of the value of global property (Savills, 2023).

Property wealth, however, is highly concentrated. The value of residential property in ten countries (China, US, Japan, Germany, UK, France, South Korea, Canada, Italy, and Australia) accounts for 75% of the global residential property market (Savills, 2021). China alone holds 26% of the global value in 2022, followed by the US at 19% (Savills, 2023). There appears to be a clear correlation between property wealth and political and economic power.

## 2.5. Personal and household debts

A growth of homeownership contributes to rising household debt, because many people need to borrow to buy a property. In the US and the UK, the average price of a property is more than 8 times the average salary. Many people therefore need to borrow to buy a property. In the UK, 70% of property purchases are funded by a mortgage (UK Finance, 2019, p. 3).

As Table 2.1 shows, the US has the highest level of mortgage debt, with the value of mortgage loans standing at $12.44 trillion in March 2024, followed by China at $5.6 trillion, UK ($2.12 trillion),

**Table 2.1** *Property values, mortgage debt, and loan-to-value ratio*

| Countries | Value of property (US$ trillion) | Value of mortgage debt (US$ trillion) | Loan to value |
|---|---|---|---|
| China | $113.50 | $5.60 | 5 |
| US | $46.60 | $12.44 | 26.7 |
| Japan | $24.73 | $1.46 | 5.9 |
| UK | $10.99 | $2.12 | 19.3 |
| Germany | N/A | $1.82 | |
| Australia | $6.24 | $0.93 | 14.9 |
| France | N/A | $0.20 | |

*Sources:* China: Dai and Chen (2024), Rapoza (2023); USA: Krechevsky (2023), Federal Reserve Bank of New York (2024), Rosen (2023); Japan: Hori (2022); UK: Neate (2023); Australia: Dervisevic (2023)

Japan ($1.46 trillion), and Australia ($0.93 trillion). Homeowners also have a lower amount of equity, with mortgage loans representing 26.7% of the US property value, in comparison with 19% in the UK and 5%–9.3% in China. This means that on average, homeowners in the US have a lower amount of equity/wealth in their homes and are more leveraged than their counterparts in the UK and China. It is feared that a significant rise in unemployment could prevent some households from keeping up with mortgage payments and force some into financial difficulties and delinquency. This could lead to a glut of housing supply while causing homelessness (Moody's Analytics, 2019, p. 6). This raises fears of a repeat of the crisis of 2007 when mortgage payment difficulties contributed to the origins of the financial crisis.

In China, the ratio of mortgage debt to property value is low. In fact, only 35% of property purchases are funded by a mortgage, and 65% buy with cash. A few years earlier, Forbes reported that in 2016 only 18% of Chinese households had a mortgage and more than 80% owned their property outright (Shepard, 2016). There are several reasons why property financing is lower in China. Chinese households save more (30% of their income), and they receive the assistance from the government (e.g. Housing Provident Fund is a government initiated savings plan with contributions matched by employers to help buy a house). However, the biggest advantage Chinese buyers have is their ability to draw upon their familial and friend networks to assist them with the house purchase. One buyer put down a deposit of roughly US$20,000, of which $3,300

(16.5%) came from her parents, $10,000 (50%) came in the form of loans from her sister and friends, and the rest (33.5%) came from her savings. In China, parents often provide a large portion of their savings to help their children buy a property. In a culture where parents often move in with their children in old age, buying a property in their son's or daughter's name is an investment in their future. Home buying in China is a multi-generational affair (Shepard, 2016).

The surge in housing prices has led many young adults, in other countries, to seek financial help from their parents for a deposit. In the UK, the Bank of Mum and Dad is expected to provide a total of £25 billion to almost half a million first-time buyers, or one in two first-time buyers, between 2022–2024 (Savills, 2022). To raise this money, parents may need to take equity from their home, use their savings, or dip into their pension fund. This in turn may affect their well-being and resources for retirement.

The scale of borrowing to buy properties is a cause of concern because it is driving up global household debt. In the US, 70% of household debt relates to mortgage debt in March 2024 ($12.44 out of $17.69 trillion) (Federal Reserve Bank of New York, 2024). In China, two-thirds of household debt is related to mortgage debt (Han et al., 2019). Australia's household debt is also closely linked with the property market. In the UK, nearly 90% of household debt is linked to property debt. In March 2024, for example, secured or mortgage debt comprised 88% of total household debt (£1.62 trillions out of £1.84 trillions) (The Money Charity, 2024, p. 5).

A large proportion of the UK population has debts – it is reported that 63% of UK adults have personal debt (Strugar, 2023). A high percentage of national wealth (67% or £8.6 trillion of £12.8 trillion) in the UK is also tied up in property. In China, 70% of household wealth is also held in property (Gao and Zaharia, 2023). The concentration of household wealth in property raises concerns because the illiquid nature of housing means that it is not easy to turn it into money if homeowners need to access their wealth to spend. In addition, the downturn in the property market can have a profound impact on the economy and the wealth of households. The case of China makes plain this point. In China, a buyer puts down 1.5 million yuan (£163,000) as a deposit for an apartment, but property prices have been falling and her flat falls in value by 14%. This affects her lifestyle and her spending: "We don't buy new clothes anymore and we don't go out. It feels like we've bought a prison for ourselves" (Gao and Zaharia, 2023). Economists call it the wealth effect: asset owners who feel poor after a sharp fall in prices tend to cut down on spending to rebuild their fortunes.

Mortgage debt has a varying impact on different age groups. Those groups most worried about debt are those between ages 25–54, partly because a high percentage of people in this age group have a mortgage and other pressing financial commitments, such as raising a family or supporting adult children and elderly parents. According to the FCA Financial Lives Survey, the age groups with the highest proportion with a mortgage are those between 35–44, followed by 45–54, and 25–34, as shown in Figure 2.3.

Figure 2.3 also shows that debt tends to decrease with age, and the highest proportion of people owning their property outright are those aged 65 and over. However, not all individuals over 65 are debt free, and a noticeable percentage has a mortgage debt in retirement and beyond the age of 75.

Research shows that many people over 55 are worried about debt, as some have unsecured and mortgage debt. A survey by Aviva in May 2023 shows that many are stressed about debt, including credit or store card debt (30% of people over 55), personal loans (16%), overdrafts (15%), and unpaid household or utility bills (10%). More than one in ten (11%) of the over-55 age group also have mortgage debt. As Aviva has

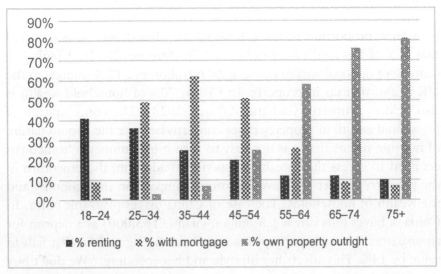

**Figure 2.3** *Housing tenure by age*
*Source:* FCA, 2021, p. 46

rightly pointed out, this debt can have a significant impact on retirement plans and financial security as it can lead to increased stress and reduced income in retirement (Aviva, 2023).

The number of people approaching retirement with mortgage debt is becoming more common. Although many people in the UK aspire to pay off their mortgage when they reach their 50s, allowing them then to focus on saving for retirement, societal changes mean that mortgages are being paid off much later in life. Higher property prices, for example, mean that it now takes longer to save for a necessary deposit and earn enough to qualify for a mortgage. Higher education also means that many people are starting their career later. A survey carried out by Hargreaves Lansdown in May 2023 shows that the average age when individuals expect to pay off their mortgage in the UK is 60 years (Taberner, 2023).

However, a growing number of borrowers do not expect to be mortgage free until well into their 70s. Indeed, a report by UK Finance shows that 52% of mortgages taken out in 2021 will go beyond the borrower's 65th birthday, and a small number beyond the age of 75 (Which, 2021).

There are three main reasons why individuals still have a mortgage in retirement. One is that first-time buyers are buying much later, with the average age of 34. More people are engaging in higher education and start their working lives later. Due to high property prices, they are also borrowing for longer to make the monthly mortgage payment more affordable. In the past, mortgages were often repaid over 25 years, but now a 30- and 40-year mortgage term is more common. If the average age of first-time buyers is 34, it means that borrowers will not be mortgage free until 64 or 74.

A second reason is a rising rate of divorce, forcing individuals to take out a new mortgage later in life. The divorce rate in the UK is estimated at 42%. The average length of marriage in the UK at the time of divorce for opposite-sex couples is 11.9 years, and the average UK divorce age for women is 43.9 and 46.4 for men. Divorce not only has an emotional impact on a couple but also affects their finances, with an average spend of nearly £15,000 on legal fees (ONS, 2022; Knibbs, 2023).

With an average divorce age of 45, starting again often means taking out a new mortgage (Hughes, 2020). If divorcees take out a new 25-year mortgage, their mortgage is not paid off until the age of 70. However, borrowers can borrow for longer to make their mortgage payments more affordable. With some lenders having a maximum age of 85 years, borrowers aged 45 can still apply for a 40-year term mortgage. Lending into retirement has become more common.

Traditionally, a low-cost option is for one spouse to remain in the family home, but they usually have to find the money to buy the other's share of the equity. If their joint mortgage is on a low-rate fixed deal, the departing spouse might feel aggrieved of having to borrow at a higher rate to buy their own property. If there is no option but to sell, both parties have to borrow at a higher rate to buy their own property, and they might have to pay an early repayment charge (Russell, 2023).

A third driving force is the growing demand from borrowers aged 55 or over, who wish to access equity or wealth from their homes. There are two ways to release wealth from a property: 1) obtain a lifetime mortgage or 2) sell part of a property. A lifetime mortgage is a loan secured on a residential property and repayable on 'exit' (death; move to a care home; voluntary repayment) rather than at a fixed maturity date. In the United Kingdom (UK), loans are advanced as a lump sum, or through flexible drawdown facilities. This is a popular way to release equity because the borrower still owns the property and might benefit from an increase in its value.

Loan interest is generally at a fixed rate but can be variable or vary subject to a cap. Interest usually 'rolls up' – that is, added to the loan. This means the amount owed grows at a compound rate, so that the final repayment is larger than the amount borrowed. This reduces the possibility of leaving an inheritance. The accruing nature of the interest leads to the use of the term 'reverse mortgage' in some territories. In the UK, there is often a guarantee that the value of the mortgage does not exceed the sale value of the property, known as a 'no negative equity guarantee' (NNEG).

A home reversion plan is different from a lifetime mortgage because it involves an individual selling a portion of their home but retaining the right to live there rent-free. Under this plan, homeowners give up ownership and the right to any future increase in the value of the property. When they die or enter long-term care, their house will be sold, and the home reversion provider will receive their proceeds.

Research into the equity release markets in 11 countries in Europe, as well as the USA and Australia, shows that over $15 billion of equity is released per year by homeowners, but by 2031, the global equity release market is expected to increase more than threefold, to more than $50 billion in annual releases (NRMLA, 2021).

Popular reasons for individuals to take out equity from their homes include home or garden improvements, holiday, supporting other members of the family, fund retirement costs, and paying off debt. Research by Age Partnership shows that £1.7 billion was released between July and September 2022, and 37% of those surveyed used the money to pay off their mortgage (Age Partnership, 2023). Using equity release means that a borrower does not have to worry about mortgage payments, as interest is rolled up and the debt is normally repaid on death. However, this will reduce their ability to leave an inheritance.

## 2.6. Mortgage and financial stress

Mortgages are often the largest financial obligations that individuals and families face during their lifetimes. A mortgage is a type of loan used to finance the purchase of a home, with the property itself serving as collateral for the loan. As a result, the stakes are high – if you're unable to make your mortgage payments, you risk losing your home through repossession when a lender takes back your home which is offered as a security. The fear of not being able to keep up with mortgage payments can cause financial stress for homeowners with a mortgage.

Financial stress related to mortgages can have a significant impact on our daily lives. Housing expenses, including mortgages, are one of the primary reasons middle-class families face financial difficulties (Warren and Tyagi, 2004). According to the American Psychological Association's 'Stress in America' survey (2019), 60% of Americans saw money as a significant source of stress (American Psychological Association, 2019, p. 6). Financial strain, including debt and housing costs, is associated with increased psychological distress and sleep disturbances (Drentea, 2000). Financial stress can also contribute to relationship issues, substance abuse, and mental health problems (Sweet et al., 2013).

According to Bullock (governor of the Reserve Bank of Australia), there are three levels of financial stress:

- Level 1: the stress is relatively mild and involves homeowners cutting back on some discretionary expenditure (such as a holiday or eating out) so that they can meet their mortgage commitments,
- Level 2: financial stress is more serious as homeowners may not be able to pay their bills and mortgages on time, resulting in mortgage arrears, which in turn affects their credit rating,

- Level 3: financial stress is severe, with households unable to meet mortgage payments and face the risk of repossession or bankruptcy. When mortgage payments exceed 30% of a household income, mortgage payments are regarded as unsustainable and are likely to push households into financial difficulties.

(Bullock, 2018, p. 7)

Evidence shows that the number of households experiencing Level 3 financial stress is relatively low, but a high percentage of households suffer Level 1 and Level 2 financial stress. In the UK, for example, there were around 90,700 mortgages in arrears and 1,100 repossessions at the end of June 2023 (Cromarty, 2023, p. 6). However, the FCA reports that 16.5 million adults were struggling with bills in January 2023 and 28.4 million people (or one in two adults) feeling anxious and stressed about the rising costs of living (FCA, 2023).

Like the UK, only a small proportion of total mortgages results in repossessions (0.23% in 2022) in the USA, but a high proportion of the population suffers from financial stress (74% with 61% live from paycheck to paycheck in September 2023). However, homeowners appear to experience a lower level of financial stress than those who do not own a home (Gupta, 2023; CNBC, 2023; Dhue and Epperson, 2023). It is possible that lower monthly housing costs, potential access to housing

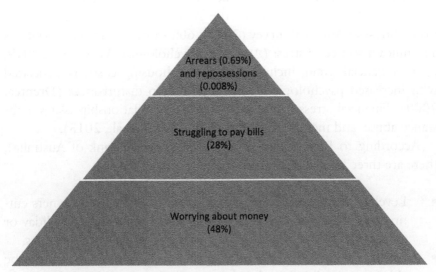

**Figure 2.4** *Different types of financial stress*
*Source:* FCA, 2023

equity in times of need (Yee and Tanzi, 2023), along with the feeling of control that homeownership confers, contribute to a lower level of financial stress.

## 2.7. Mortgage insomnia and psychological well-being

Mortgage insomnia is a term used to describe the sleep disturbances, anxiety, and stress caused by the financial burden of dealing with a home loan. It refers to the worry and restlessness that many homeowners experience due to the long-term commitment, high interest rates, and other factors associated with mortgages. It is difficult to provide an exact number of people impacted by mortgage insomnia, as this term is not widely used in academic literature, and studies on this specific issue are limited. However, we can examine the prevalence of financial stress related to housing, which contributes to mortgage insomnia.

Several studies find the link between stress and poor sleep quality – Hall et al. (2000), for example, argues that insomnia is associated with stress, while Hicks and Garcia (1987) found that the greater the level of stress, the less time spent asleep. The stress-sleep cycle is illustrated in Figure 2.5, which highlights the interaction between stress, lack of sleep, tiredness, ability to cope with daily life, and low esteem. However, it is recognised that everyone reacts to stress differently, and there is not one universal response.

Housing debt can have a significant impact on mental health and well-being due to the financial stress and long-term commitment they entail. The burden of mortgage payments and concerns about meeting these obligations can lead to anxiety, depression, and sleep disturbances, which in turn affect overall well-being. Individuals with high levels of housing debt reported lower levels of psychological well-being compared to those with lower levels of debt. These findings suggest that mortgages can negatively impact mental health (Brown et al., 2005). In the UK, research by the Office of National Statistics finds that those who are behind on energy bills or borrow more than usual suffer from high levels of reported anxiety, and lower levels of life satisfaction, happiness, and feelings that things done in life are worthwhile (ONS, 2023).

A substantial link has also been observed between heightened levels of debt and thoughts of suicide, notably in individuals dealing with mortgage arrears. This indicates that housing debt might play a significant role as a risk factor for considering suicide (Meltzer et al., 2011). Housing

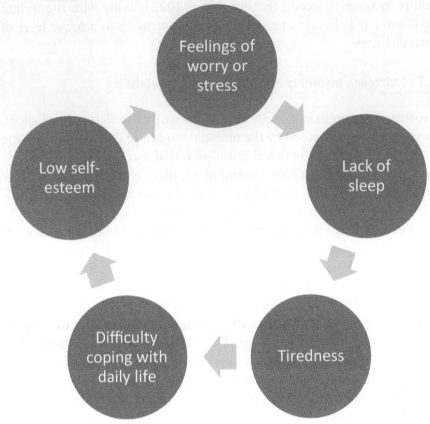

**Figure 2.5** *Stress-sleep cycle*
*Source:* Adapted from MIND, 2024

debt can also contribute to feelings of hopelessness and helplessness, leading to a higher risk of suicidal behaviour. Ongoing financial stress related to mortgage obligations may cause individuals to feel trapped and overwhelmed, exacerbating mental health issues and increasing the risk of suicide (Roelfs and Shor, 2023).

The level of psychological distress and financial stress are influenced by types of housing tenure: renting, owning with mortgage, and owning without a mortgage. Cairney and Boyle (2004) argue that the stress level is highest for renters, lower for homeowners with a mortgage, and lowest for those without a mortgage. Therefore, achieving a debt-free status positively impacts our well-being. Homeowners with no mortgage debt live longer, display superior physical and mental health, and require fewer health services compared to renters and those with mortgages, as they experience reduced psychological distress and depression (Miranda et al.,

2017) This is not surprising, as mortgage free means the elimination of the biggest monthly expense and increased disposable income, giving unencumbered homeowners not only more money to enjoy life but also a sense of financial security and confidence without worrying about earning money to pay their mortgage to keep a roof over their head.

## 2.8. Conclusion

A mortgage is often one of the most substantial financial commitments we undertake in our lives, playing a pivotal role in shaping our overall financial well-being. The shift in lifecycle – later career start, later first-time home purchase, bigger debt, and later paying off mortgage – means that debt is carried over a longer period of time and into retirement, affecting the quality of life and psychological well-being of working individuals and retirees.

Yet, there are few guides available to help us develop strategies to repay our mortgage off early. In the following chapters, we will discuss the pros and cons of paying off your mortgage early, before moving on to examine key strategies that can be adopted to accelerate an early repayment. By gaining an insight into this important topic, we can better navigate our financial journey, make informed decisions, and ultimately work towards achieving financial stability and peace of mind for ourselves and our families.

## References

Age Partnership. (2023) The reason for releasing equity in homes is changing. Available at: www.agepartnership.co.uk/media-centre/equity-release/reason-for-release/ [Accessed 12 July 2023].

American Psychological Association. (2019). Stress in America. Available at: www.apa.org/news/press/releases/stress/2019/stress-america-2019.pdf [Accessed 12 July 2023].

Aviva. (2023). More than 1 in 10 over 55s have mortgage debt in the run up to retirement. Available at: www.aviva.com/newsroom/news-releases/2023/05/more-than-1-in-10-over-55s-have-mortgage-debt-in-the-run-up-to-retirement/ [Accessed 12 July 2023].

Brown, S., Taylor, K., and Wheatley Price, S. (2005). Debt and distress: Evaluating the psychological cost of credit. *Journal of Economic Psychology*, 26 (5), 642–663. Available at: www.academia.edu/18374914/Debt_and_distress_Evaluating_the_psychological_cost_of_credit [Accessed 12 July 2023].

Bullock, M. (2018). Household indebtedness and mortgage stress. Available at: www.bis.org/review/r180226e.pdf [Accessed 12 July 2023].

Cairney, J., and Boyle, M. H. (2004). Home ownership, mortgages and psychological distress. *Housing Studies*, 19 (2), 161–174. https://doi.org/10.1080/0267303032000168577. Available at: www.tandfonline.com/doi/abs/10.1080/0267303032000168577 [Accessed 12 July 2023].

CNBC. (2023). Majority of Americans feeling financially stressed and living paycheck to paycheck. *CNBC*. Available at: www.cnbc.com/2023/09/07/majority-of-americans-feeling-financially-stressed-and-living-paycheck-to-paycheck-according-to-cnbc-your-money-survey.html [Accessed 12 October 2023].

Cromarty, H. (2023). Mortgage arrears and repossessions in England. *House of Commons Library*. Available at: https://researchbriefings.files.parliament.uk/documents/SN04769/SN04769.pdf [Accessed 7 October 2023].

Dai, X., and Chen, Y. (2024). China's property market downturn: The risk of global contagion. *Swiss Re Institute*. Available at: www.swissre.com/institute/research/sigma-research/Economic-Insights/china-property-market.html [Accessed 23 January 2024].

Dervisevic, H. (2023). Australian housing market tops $10 trillion for the second time. Available at: www.savings.com.au/news/corelogic-housing-market-ten-trillion [Accessed 23 January 2024].

Dhue, S., and Epperson, S. (2023). 70% of Americans are feeling financially stressed. *CNBC*. Available at: www.cnbc.com/2023/04/11/70percent-of-americans-feel-financially-stressed-new-cnbc-survey-finds.html [Accessed 7 October 2023].

Drentea, P. (2000). Age, debt and anxiety. *Journal of Health and Social Behavior*, 41 (4), 437–450. https://doi.org/10.2307/2676296

Equity Release Council. (2021). Home advantage: Intergenerational perspectives on property wealth in later life. Available at: www.equityreleasecouncil.com/wp-content/uploads/2021/08/Equity-Release-Council-Home-advantage-intergenerational-report-August-2021-FINAL.pdf [Accessed 12 July 2023].

Eurostat. (2023). House or flat – owning or renting. Available at: https://ec.europa.eu/eurostat/cache/digpub/housing/bloc-1a.html [Accessed 12 July 2023].

FCA. (2021). Financial Lives 2020 survey: The impact of coronavirus. Available at: https://www.fca.org.uk/publication/research/financial-lives-survey-2020.pdf [Accessed 8 June 2024].

FCA. (2023). Financial Lives January 2023. Available at: www.fca.org.uk/publications/financial-lives/financial-lives-january-2023-consumer-experience [Accessed 7 October 2023].

Federal Reserve Bank of New York. (2024). Household debt rose by $184 billion in Q1 2024. Available at: https://www.newyorkfed.org/newsevents/news/research/2024/20240514 [Accessed 15 June 2024].

Gao, L., and Zaharia, M. (2023). Feeling poorer: Property slump hurting Chinese consumers, clouding recovery. *Reuters*. Available at: www.reuters.com/markets/asia/feeling-poorer-property-slump-hurting-chinese-consumers-clouds-recovery-2023-04-14/#:~:text=In%20play%20now%20in%20China,prominent%20driver%20of%20economic%20growth [Accessed 12 July 2023].

Gupta, R. (2023). US foreclosure rate by year, state and city. *Finmasters*. Available at: https://finmasters.com/foreclosure-rate/#gref [Accessed 12 October 2023].

Hall, M., Buysse, D. J., Nowell, P. D., Nofzinger, E. A., Houck, P., Reynolds 3rd, C. F., Kupfer, D. J. (2000). Symptoms of stress and depression as correlates of sleep in primary insomnia. *Psychosomatic Medicine*, 62 (2), 227–230.

Han, F., Jurzyk, E., Guo, W., He, Y., and Rendak, N. (2019). Assessing macro-financial risks of household debt in China. IMF Working Paper Asia and Pacific Department. Available at: www.imf.org/-/media/Files/Publications/WP/2019/wpiea2019258-print-pdf.ashx [Accessed 12 July 2023].

HDFC. (2023). 9 advantages buying a home over renting. Available at: www.hdfc.com/blog/property-and-real-estate/9-advantages-buying-home-renting [Accessed 12 July 2023].

Hicks, R. A., and Garcia, E. R. (1987). Level of stress and sleep duration. *Perceptual and Motor Skills*, 64 (1). Available at: https://journals.sagepub.com/doi/10.2466/pms.1987.64.1.44 [Accessed 12 July 2023].

Hori, D. (2022). Japan mortgage balances soar despite slowing property values. *Asia Nikkei*. Available at: https://asia.nikkei.com/Spotlight/Datawatch/Japan-mortgage-balances-soar-despite-slowing-property-values#:~:text=TOKYO%20%2D%2D%20The%20outstanding%20balance,climbed%20faster%20than%20mortgage%20liabilities [Accessed 23 January 2024].

Huang, Y., He, S., and Gan, L. (2021). Introduction to SI: Homeownership and housing divide in China. Available at: www.ncbi.nlm.nih.gov/pmc/articles/PMC7546956/#:~:text=Today%20China%20is%20a%20country,et%20al.%2C%20 2020) [Accessed 12 July 2023].

Hughes, K. (2020). Expect to still be paying off your mortgage in old age, homeowners warned. Available at: www.independent.co.uk/money/mortgage-debt-coronavirus-house-prices-costs-b689516.html [Accessed 12 July 2023].

Juwai. (2017). Why are Chinese so obsessed with buying property? Available at: https://list.juwai.com/news/2017/06/why-are-chinese-so-obsessed-with-buying-property [Accessed 12 July 2023].

Knibbs, J. (2023). London and UK's divorce hotspots revealed: new data shows how many marriages and partnerships breakup. *Evening Standard*. Available at: www.standard.co.uk/news/uk/most-divorces-london-uk-census-data-b1062398.html [Accessed 12 July 2023].

Krechevsky, D. (2023). Redfin: $2.3T in home values lost in 2nd Half of '22. *National Mortgage Professional*, 22 February. Available at: https://nationalmortgage-professional.com/news/redfin-23t-home-values-lost-2nd-half-22 [Accessed 9 June 2024].

Meltzer, H., Bebbington, P., Brugha, T., Jenkins, R., McManus, S., and Stansfeld, S. (2011). Personal debt and suicidal ideation. *Psychological Medicine*, 41 (4), 771–778. Available at: www.researchgate.net/publication/44675779_Personal_debt_and_suicidal_ideation#fullTextFileContent [Accessed 12 July 2023].

MIND. (2023). How to cope with sleep problems. Available at: www.mind.org.uk/information-support/types-of-mental-health-problems/sleep-problems/about-sleep-and-mental-health/ [Accessed 12 July 2023].

Miranda, P. Y., Reyes, A., Hudson, D., Yao, N., Bleser, W. K., Snipes, S. A., and BeLue, R. (2017). Reports of self-rated health by citizenship and homeownership, United States 2000–2010. *Preventive Medicine*, 100, 3–9.

Moldovan, I. (2018). The country where 96% of homes are privately owned. *BBC*. Available at: www.bbc.com/worklife/article/20181119-the-country-where-96-of-citizens-own-homes [Accessed 26 October 2023).

Moody's Analytics. (2019). Some rising pressure points in global debt. Available at: www.moodysanalytics.com/-/media/article/2018/global-debt.pdf [Accessed 12 July 2023].

Munford, L.A., Fichera, E., and Sutton, M. (2020). Is owning your home good for your health? Evidence from exogenous variations in subsidies in England. *Economics & Human Biology*, 39. Available at: www.sciencedirect.com/science/article/pii/S1570677X20301738#:~:text=Longer%20commuting%20times%2C%20which%20may,health%20through%20better%20housing%20conditions [Accessed 12 July 2023].

Neate, R. (2023). Value of UK housing stock hit record £8.7 trillion in 2022. *Guardian*. Available at: www.theguardian.com/money/2023/feb/27/total-value-of-uk-housing-stock-record-868tn-2022-fall-house-prices-2023#:~:text=The%20total%20value%20of%20all,425bn%20on%20a%20year%20earlier [Accessed 23 January 2024].

Nettleton, S., and Burrows, R. (1998). Mortgage debt, insecure home ownership and health: An exploratory analysis. *Sociology of Health & Illness*, 20 (5), 731–753. Available at: https://onlinelibrary.wiley.com/doi/pdf/10.1111/1467-9566.00127 [Accessed 12 July 2023].

New Economics Foundation (NEF). (2015). The financialisation of UK homes: The housing crisis, land, and the banks. Available at: https://neweconomics.org/uploads/files/496c07a5b30026d43a_d1m6i26iy.pdf [Accessed 7 October 2023].

NRMLA. (2021). Global equity release market forecast to more than Treble by 2031. Available at: www.nrmlaonline.org/2021/01/29/global-equity-release-market-forecast-to-more-than-treble-by-2031 [Accessed 12 July 2023].

ONS. (2022). Divorce in England and Wales. Available at: www.ons.gov.uk/peoplepopulationandcommunity/birthsdeathsandmarriages/divorce/bulletins/divorcesinenglandandwales/2021 [Accessed 12 July 2023].

ONS. (2023). How are financial pressures affecting people in Great Britain? Available at: www.ons.gov.uk/peoplepopulationandcommunity/wellbeing/articles/howarefinancialpressuresaffectingpeopleingreatbritain/2023-02-22 [Accessed 12 July 2023].

Rapoza, K. (2023). China's 'debt crisis' gets Washington hearing after Evergrande Bust. *Forbes*. Available at: www.forbes.com/sites/kenrapoza/2023/08/21/chinas-debt-crisis-gets-washington-hearing-after-evergrande-bust/?sh=39aec36129a3 [Accessed 23 January 2024].

Roelfs, D. J., and Shor, E. (2023). Financial stress, unemployment, and suicide – A meta-analysis. *Crisis: The Journal of Crisis Intervention and Suicide Prevention*, 44 (6), 506–517.

Rosen, P. (2023). The US housing market hits a record value of $47 trillion as the inventory shortage fuels a price boom. *Business Insider*. Available at: https://markets.businessinsider.com/news/commodities/housing-market-inventory-shortage-home-prices-value-real-estate-property-2023-8 [Accessed 16 June 2024].

Russell, B. (2023). Mortgage crisis complicates the property conundrum for separating couples. *IFA Magazine*. Available at: https://ifamagazine.com/mortgage-crisis-complicates-the-property-conundrum-for-separating-couples/ [Accessed 12 July 2023].

Santander. (2019). Santander first-time buyer study: The future of the homeownership dream. Available at: www.santander.co.uk/assets/s3fs-public/documents/santander-first-time-buyer-study.pdf [Accessed 12 July 2023].

Savills. (2021). Value of global real estate rises 5% to $326.5 trillion. Available at: www.savills.co.uk/insight-and-opinion/savills-news/319145-0/value-of-global-real-estate-rises-5-to-$326.5-trillion [Accessed 12 July 2023].

Savills. (2022). Bank of Mum & Dad to lend a total £25 billion to their children over the next three years. Available at: www.savills.co.uk/insight-and-opinion/savills-news/331423-0/bank-of-mum-and-dad-to-lend-a-total-%C2%A325-billion-to-their-children-over-the-next-three-years [Accessed 12 July 2023].

Savills. (2023). Total value of global real estate: Property remains the world's biggest store of wealth. *Savills*. Available at: www.savills.com/impacts/market-trends/the-total-value-of-global-real-estate-property-remains-the-worlds-biggest-store-of-wealth.html [Accessed 19 October 2023].

Shepard, W. (2016). How people in China afford their outrageously expensive homes. Available at: www.forbes.com/sites/wadeshepard/2016/03/30/how-people-in-china-afford-their-outrageously-expensive-homes [Accessed 12 July 2023].

Strugar, M. (2023) UK debt statistics. Available at: https://cybercrew.uk/blog/debt-statistics-uk/#:~:text=As%20of%20November%202021%2C%20the,is%20facing%20a%20debt%20problem [Accessed 12 July 2023].

Sweet, E., Nandi, A., Adam, E. K., and McDade, T. W. (2013). The high price of debt: household financial debt and its impact on mental and physical health. Available at: https://pubmed.ncbi.nlm.nih.gov/23849243/ [Accessed 12 July 2023].

Taberner, P. (2023). More than one in six people will still be paying off mortgages over the age of 65. *Mortgage Solutions*. Available at: www.mortgagesolutions.co.uk/news/2023/06/26/more-than-one-in-six-people-will-still-be-paying-off-mortgages-over-the-age-of-65/#:~:text=The%20average%20age%20when%20you,higher%20interest%20rates%20on%20mortgages [Accessed 12 July 2023].

The Money Charity. (2024). Money statistics May 2024. Available at: https://themoneycharity.org.uk/media/May-2024-Money-Statistics.pdf [Accessed 15 June 2024].

UK Finance. (2019). The changing shape of the UK mortgage market. Available at: www.ukfinance.org.uk/system/files/The-changing-shape-of-the-UK-mortgage-market-FINAL-ONLINE-Jan-2020.pdf [Accessed 12 July 2023].

Warren, E., and Warren Tyagi, A. (2004). *The Two-Income Trap: Why Middle-Class Parents Are Going Broke*. New York: Basic Books.

Which. (2021). Over half of borrowers will still have a mortgage at 65: how to pay off your home loan more quickly. Available at: www.which.co.uk/news/article/over-half-of-borrowers-will-still-have-a-mortgage-at-65-how-to-pay-off-your-home-loan-more-quickly-aaP9q4p2ARpk [Accessed 12 July 2023].

World Economic Forum. (2021). Rent or buy? These countries have the most renters vs. homeowners. Available at: www.weforum.org/agenda/2021/04/global-percentage-rent-own-global-property [Accessed 12 July 2023].

Yee, A., and Tanzi, A. (2023). More Americans are losing their homes as foreclosures on US properties rise. *Bloomberg*. Available at: www.bloomberg.com/news/articles/2023-04-19/foreclosures-on-us-properties-continued-to-rise-in-first-quarter [Accessed 12 October 2023].

## CHAPTER THREE

# WEIGHING THE DECISION
## PAYING OFF YOUR MORTGAGE – ADVANTAGES AND DISADVANTAGES

## 3.1. Introduction

The question of whether to pay off a mortgage early can present a big dilemma for homeowners, as benefits have to be weighed up against personal sacrifices. In this chapter, we'll discuss the advantages and disadvantages of paying off your mortgage by examining the emotional and financial trade-offs. By exploring these factors, you'll be better prepared to make a well-informed decision that suits your financial objectives and personal situation.

## 3.2. Advantages of paying off your mortgage

### 3.2.1. Save interest

A compelling reason to repay a mortgage early is to save interest payments. One homeowner calculates that for every £1 he pays to the lender, 50 pence goes to pay the interest on the loan. Over a mortgage term of 25 years, he would have to pay a total of £160,000 in interest, which is a third of the cost of his property (£440,000). Another homeowner is motivated to pay off the mortgage early after a dismayed discovery that his £5,500 payments only reduce his loan by £2,000 and £3,500 goes to pay interest.

DOI: 10.4324/9781003297765-3

Simon and Eliza bought their first house in 2010 for £155,000 and paid a 10% deposit. With a mortgage of £140,000 over 30 years at a 6% interest rate, they remember seeing the total interest on the mortgage illustration of £160,000, which is more than the cost of their house. This motivated them to repay their mortgage as soon as possible. Their monthly mortgage payment was £1,000, and when the mortgage rate fell to 2.5%, resulting in a lower monthly payment, they still maintained their initial payment. This led to overpayment, allowing them to reduce the loan amount. With only a small amount left to pay, they decided to borrow some money from their family to fully repay their mortgage in 2023. In just 13 years, they have repaid their mortgage, shortening the term by 17 years.

The financial benefits of early repayment can be illustrated below using a simple example of a loan of £100,000 on a repayment mortgage (repaying capital and interest) at a 5% interest rate. Table 3.1 demonstrates the benefits of paying off your mortgage early.

The table clearly shows the shorter the mortgage term, the lower the total interest paid. If homeowners repay the mortgage in ten years, interest payments represent 27% of the original loan. If a mortgage is repaid over 30 years, the total amount of interest will almost equal the original loan (93%), and over 40 years the amount of interest paid will be 131% of the original amount borrowed. This can be illustrated in Figure 3.1.

Paying off your mortgage early, and paying less interest, can be likened to receiving a discount on one's home: the sooner the mortgage is paid off, the larger the discount becomes. Homeowners do not have to pay off their mortgage in full to enjoy the benefits. They can overpay by paying a lump sum (as a result of receiving a bonus, inheritance, or redundancy) toward their loan balance or an extra monthly amount; both lower the overall interest costs and enable homeowners to save money.

### 3.2.2. Avoid interest rate rise risk

Homeowners with a mortgage face an interest rate rise risk – that is, the risk of interest rate rising, affecting their ability to pay their mortgage payment. This can affect all homeowners with a mortgage, especially those on variable rates and those coming to the end of a fixed mortgage deal. This can cause sleepless nights and stress, as illustrated by the examples below.

**Table 3.1** *Interest payments at different mortgage terms*

| Amount borrowed (£) | Term of mortgage (years) | Term of mortgage (months) | Monthly payment | Total interest payment | Interest as % of original loan |
|---|---|---|---|---|---|
| £100,000 | 10 | 120 | £1,060 | 27,300 | 27 |
| £100,000 | 15 | 180 | £791 | 42,377 | 42 |
| £100,000 | 20 | 240 | £660 | 58,437 | 58 |
| £100,000 | 25 | 300 | £585 | 75,441 | 75 |
| £100,000 | 30 | 360 | £537 | 93,338 | 93 |
| £100,000 | 35 | 420 | £505 | 112,066 | 112 |
| £100,000 | 40 | 480 | £482 | 131,568 | 131 |

*Source:* Author's calculations using Moneysavingexpert.com's Basic mortgage calculator

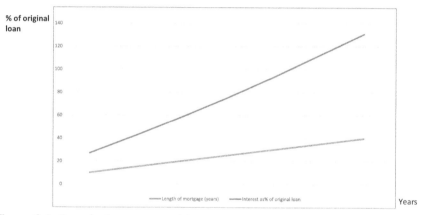

**Figure 3.1** *Length of mortgage and interest*

A couple have an interest-only mortgage and are suffering sleepless nights in the face of rising interest rates. They bought their house 20 years ago when they had two incomes and no children. Over the years they have been increasing their loan for home improvements and have £450,000 remaining. They are coming to the end of their fixed mortgage deal, and they have been experiencing sleepless nights because if the best mortgage deal they can obtain is 6% or more, they will struggle as they now only have one income but two young children to support. At a 6% mortgage rate, they calculate that they will have to find an extra £1,480 per month (nearly £18,000 a year), which is well over double what they are currently paying. They say that this is 'ruining their lives'.

Another couple chose a tracker mortgage at 0.34 percentage points above the Bank of England base rate in the hope that interest rates would fall in the coming months. Unfortunately, rates have been rising steadily, and their new interest only mortgage is £1,600 per month – three times their previous payment of £524. They have two young daughters and pay £2,300 a month in school fees. They are worried that should their interest repayments reach £2,000 a month, they will struggle to pay.

Another man has also been caught out by rapidly rising interest rates. He has a mortgage of £900,000 and has decided to sell because their five-year fixed mortgage deal has come to an end, and the new rate would be above 6%. This means that their monthly payment would rise by £2,000 a month, from £4,000 to £6,000. He and his wife are high earners and feel that they have no option but to sell and go back to renting. This would cost £4,000 a month to rent, which is still cheaper than paying for a mortgage.

One man feels lucky to have secured a relatively good deal before rates went up. He got in touch with his mortgage broker six months before his deal expired and managed to secure a five-year fixed deal at 3.6%. His monthly repayment was £2,300. At 3.6%, he would pay £1,500 per month more, or £18,000 extra a year. Although this would absorb 50% of his take-home pay, he feels lucky as at 4% he would have been forced to sell.

### 3.2.3. Avoid the risk of becoming a mortgage prisoner

Paying off your mortgage also eliminates the risk of becoming a mortgage prisoner. Mortgage prisoners refer to people who are unable to switch mortgages to a better deal because their lender is no longer active and cannot offer a new mortgage contract. The UK Mortgage Prisoners claims that there are 250,000 mortgage prisoners, and the stories of some mortgage prisoners are documented on their website (UK Mortgage Prisoners, 2023).

The FCA's Mortgage Prisoner Review in 2021 provided a detailed analysis of consumers who are unable to switch lenders. It identified 195,000 mortgage accounts with closed book lenders. Out of these, the FCA identified a cohort of 47,000 mortgage prisoners who are up to date with mortgage payments but who cannot switch providers as they do not meet current lending criteria, due to factors such as their age, income, or credit score (FCA, 2021; Browning, 2023).

One mortgage prisoner is a man, 51, who took out an interest-only mortgage for £150,000 for his semi-detached home in 2007. His current outstanding balance is £154,000. His lender was Southern Pacific Mortgage Loans, owned by the US investment bank Lehman Brothers, which went bust during the 2008 financial crisis.

His wife stopped work in 2018 due to illness, and he stopped working in 2019 to care for his wife. They had trouble paying their mortgage from the start and have been relying on charities to pay their £970 per month mortgage (at 7.55% interest). The financial struggle has affected his mental health, requiring him to take anti-depressants (Green, 2023).

His case shows that taking out an interest-only mortgage without any plan of how to pay it off is risky. A change in personal circumstances and/or declining health can affect a homeowner's ability to earn a living and pay their mortgage.

### 3.2.4. Elimination of the biggest monthly financial commitment from a household budget

A third advantage of paying off a mortgage is to reduce or eliminate the biggest monthly expense from a household's budget. Mortgage payments are often the largest monthly expense, consuming a significant proportion of income, especially for those on a low income. In 2021–2022, households with a mortgage spent on average 22% of their income on mortgage payments, in comparison to private renters who spend 38% on housing, and social renters 36% (English Housing Survey, 2022). Lower-income households spend a greater proportion of their income on their mortgage. Data available for 2019–2020 indicate that while those in the highest income category spent 13% of their income on their mortgage, those on the lowest income 47%. Spending more than 30% of income on mortgage payment is seen as a sign of housing stress. In 2019–2020, 35% of people in the bottom two income brackets spent more than 30% of their income on their housing costs (English Housing Survey, 2021, p. 20).

Figure 3.2 shows the average annual mortgage payment between 2020–2022 and that Londoners pay more for their mortgage than the rest of England. Paying off their mortgage means that homeowners can save between £8,500–£9,500 per year, while Londoners £12,000–£18,000. However, interest rates have gone up substantially since,

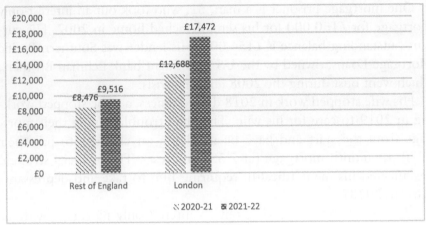

**Figure 3.2** *Average annual housing costs, 2020–2022*
*Source:* English Housing Survey, 2021–2022

and many households may be paying a lot more than the amounts indicated.

In the US, mortgage payments have increased as a result of surging interest rates. The percentage of income spent on mortgage payments, for example, rose from 19.3% in December 2020 to nearly 32% by April 2022 (Wink et al., 2022). As interest rates have gone up even further since April 2022, the percentage of income spent on mortgage payments is likely to rise further. This is likely to result in mortgage stress, as spending more than 30% of income on housing costs is regarded as unsustainable.

Paying off a mortgage and owning a property outright frees up a significant portion of a homeowner's monthly income. Without the burden of mortgage payments, homeowners would have more disposable income to allocate towards other financial goals, such as saving for retirement, investing, more holidays, better-quality food, setting up a business, or pursuing personal interests. This can contribute to a sense of financial stability, security, and well-being.

### 3.2.5. Save more for retirement

The elimination of mortgage payments from your disposable income frees up money for other uses, especially saving for retirement. If an individual has a mortgage, a percentage of their income is used to service the debt, and so less is available for saving for retirement. If they are debt free, they can channel their surplus income into a pension fund to provide an income in retirement. Paying off a mortgage by the age of 50 is ideal, allowing individuals to accelerate saving and investing for old age as they approach retirement.

However, research carried out by the Institute of Fiscal Studies shows that owner-occupiers do not increase their pension contribution when they have completely repaid their mortgage. In fact, only 5% of individuals increase their monthly private pension contributions by £150 or more as a result of completing repayment of their mortgage. In addition, the pension contributions made by these individuals are lower than average mortgage expenditure per person prior to mortgage completion (average of £344 per month).

There are a few possible explanations as to why not everyone increases their pension saving on repayment of their mortgage. Those on lower lifetime incomes might have less need to save for retirement through private pensions because state pension provides them with a greater replacement of their earnings than it does for middle and higher earners.

Alternatively, those with employer-provided private pensions may not increase their contributions because they may feel that their retirement benefits or the default contribution levels are adequate (Crawford, 2020, pp. 18–19).

In addition, it is possible that unencumbered homeowners do not increase their pension saving because they realise that, as they have paid off their mortgage and eliminated the biggest monthly expense, they require a smaller pension fund than renters. Research by ONS (2020) suggests that someone who owns a property outright could expect to maintain their living standards on a pension pot of £260,000 in the UK, while someone who rents privately would need £445,000 (ONS, 2020).

### 3.2.6. Ability to help children get a mortgage

Repaying a mortgage may enable parents to have surplus income to help support their children in applying for a mortgage. In the UK, many young children struggle to get on the property ladder because their salary is insufficient to support a mortgage loan required. They need help with their income as well as a house deposit. Lenders therefore have introduced a unique type of mortgage, known as joint mortgage sole proprietor (JMSP), whereby a parent can apply for a joint mortgage with their children. Although the mortgage is in joint names, the child remains the sole owner, and in effect, this type of mortgage allows them to add the salary of a parent to their income to allow them to borrow a higher amount.

However, the amount they can borrow is partly determined by the parent's outstanding mortgage on their main residence. This means that if the parent has no outstanding mortgage on their main home, they can help their children more by allowing them to take out a bigger loan.

### 3.2.7. Increased home equity

Increased home equity is a notable advantage of owning a property without a mortgage. Home equity refers to the difference between the market value of a property and any outstanding mortgage balance. In other words, it represents property wealth of a household. As homeowners pay off their mortgage, their home equity increases, providing them with valuable financial resources.

In the UK, property wealth was worth approximately £7 trillion in 2022, representing the difference between the value of homes of £8.7 trillion and outstanding mortgage debt of £1.7 trillion. Of this, nearly half, £3.34 trillion, was held by mortgage-free homeowners (City AM, 2023; Prosser, 2023). According to ONS (2022a), the self-employed had the highest amount of property wealth (£286,000), in comparison to the retired (£277,000) and employed (£182,000) in the period between 2018–2020. There is a great regional variation in home equity: in 2021, it is reported that London had the highest level of average equity at £178,680 per household, South East £126,278, East Anglia £108,732, in comparison with North East (£54,489) and Yorkshire (£65,385) (Today's Conveyancer, 2021).

In the US, homeowners are reported to enjoy $300,000 of equity in 2022 but falling house prices at the beginning of 2023 led to a slump in housing equity to $274,000. However, this is still higher than the

 **MINUS**       **EQUAL**

Value of property          Mortgage balance          Housing wealth / equity

**Figure 3.3** *Housing wealth equity*

amount of equity before the pandemic of $182,000 (Hansen, 2022; Bankrate, 2023). As a nation, Americans are reported to have a total home equity of US$28.7 trillion with tappable equity (amount available to lend or borrow against while keeping a 20% equity cushion) of US$9.3 trillion (Ballentine and Cachero, 2023).

Equity or wealth in the home can be accessed in two ways: take out a new mortgage at a higher value or apply for an additional loan which is secured on top of an existing mortgage. Taking out a new mortgage with a new lender is often a cheaper option, but homeowners may not be able or want to do so as they may have a mortgage deal which imposes a financial penalty for repaying early, or they may enjoy a low rate on their current mortgage which they would lose if they change their mortgage.

Homeowners who want to access their home equity but unable to change their main mortgage can do so by taking out an additional loan (known as a second charge or secured loan in the UK and Heloc in the US). This is more expensive than a normal mortgage because the second lender receives a lower priority than the first mortgage lender (known as first charge) in the event a property has to be repossessed and sold to repay the debt. However, it is still cheaper than other forms of unsecured loans such as personal loans or credit cards, as the second charge lender also holds the property as a collateral. In the US, Heloc loans rose by 34% in 2022, with more than 1.41 million individual loans (Ballentine and Cachero, 2023).

Homeowners access their home equity for several reasons. First, education expenses can be significant, and many parents seek various funding sources to support their children's education, to help cover tuition fees, books, and other related costs. In the US, for example, a couple bought a house in 2018 for US$560,000. Four years later, their home was worth US$1 million, and so in March 2022 they took out a loan secured on their property, or a Heloc, to pay for repairs of an investment property and their children's Montessori school fees (Ballentine and Cachero, 2023).

Second, as individuals approach retirement, having substantial home equity serves as an essential financial resource. Homeowners can use their equity to supplement their retirement income by downsizing to a smaller property, opting for a reverse mortgage, or even selling the property and investing the proceeds.

Additionally, increased home equity provides homeowners with the opportunity to make improvements or renovations to their property, which can enhance its value, improve living conditions, and contribute to the overall enjoyment of the home. For homeowners with multiple high-interest debts, such as credit cards or personal loans, leveraging home equity can be a strategic way to consolidate and pay off these debts. This may allow them to secure lower interest rates and simplify their monthly payments. However, there are two potential downsides. First, this can increase the risk of losing their home, because they are effectively giving lenders their home as a collateral by turning unsecured debt (e.g. credit card and personal loans) into secured debt (e.g. mortgage). Second, they can end up paying more interest as a mortgage is often repaid over a longer period of time than other forms of borrowing.

Furthermore, with increased home equity, homeowners have the option to invest in various financial opportunities, such as starting a business, purchasing rental properties, or investing in stocks and bonds. In the US, one man bought a house in 2014 for US$400,000 but this has doubled in value. In February 2023, he took out a Heloc for US$200,000 at 9% interest rate with the intention of buying properties to rent out. However, he was struggling to find properties that give him sufficient yield to make it worthwhile, but he likes to have access to the cash if he needs it. Another man took out a Heloc in May 2022 for US$50,000 line of credit on his flat to buy a property but has not been able to do so. While waiting for a suitable property, he uses the money to trade stocks and shares. He says that the profit he makes on the trades is enough to pay the interest on the Heloc (Ballentine and Cachero, 2023).

In other words, home equity can be accessed to provide flexibility and liquidity and pay for a wide range of financial needs, including a new car, school fees, or alleviation of financial pressures (Prosser, 2023).

### 3.2.8. Financial stability and security

Financial stability plays a crucial role in an individual's well-being. When homeowners pay off their mortgage, they gain not only complete ownership of their property but also financial stability, security, and peace of mind. After paying off their mortgage, for example, Simon and Eliza remember feeling 'wow, amazing', and feel that at last their house is now 'their home'. They would welcome guests to '*our*' home. This achievement contributes to a sense of financial security and can have a positive impact on their overall quality of life.

One key benefit of financial stability is the reduction of stress and anxiety associated with keeping up with monthly mortgage payments. Homeowners who no longer have this obligation can experience reduced stress levels, as they do not have to worry about meeting and keeping up with mortgage payment deadlines, facing potential penalties for late or missed payments, or rising mortgage rates that would have affected their budget and lifestyle. This sense of relief can translate into improved mental health and well-being. Some people do not like debt, and being burdened with debt causes them financial anxiety, especially in times of economic uncertainty, like what we are experiencing now with rising interest rates and costs of living. Therefore, paying off debt faster or fully reduces financial anxiety and improves general feelings of happiness and mental well-being.

### 3.2.9. Financial security for family in the event of premature death

Paying off a mortgage also increases financial security for family members in the event of death. As Figure 3.4 shows, surviving family members of homeowners with no mortgage or who have paid their mortgage off enjoy financial security and do not have to worry about being made homeless because there is no debt on their home.

Surviving members of homeowners with a life insurance face some financial uncertainty because it might take some time for an insurance policy to pay out, especially if a life insurance policy is not set up correctly (i.e. not put in a trust or joint ownership to avoid probate delays).

However, surviving members of homeowners with no life insurance face a high level of uncertainty and worry about the future of their housing as there is no insurance payout to repay the mortgage. In this difficult time, they may have to consider selling their home, moving in with relatives, or selling quickly at a reduced price to settle the debt (Corden et al., 2008, pp. 106–108).

**Figure 3.4** *Mortgage debt, life insurance and impact on survivors*

Years ago, a client of the author died, leaving behind a widow and three young sons. They had a £500,000 mortgage but only £100,000 of life insurance cover. As this was insufficient to pay off the debt, the widow had to sell their family home and move into a smaller buy-to-let property they owned. It is therefore important to regularly review protection needs to ensure that the level of life insurance at least matches the level of debt. This will give survivors the financial security they need, and the time and the space to grieve.

### 3.2.10. Life choices

Being mortgage free gives homeowners lifestyle choices, especially as they get older. When individuals approach their 50s, many may wish to reduce their working hours, stop working, or become unable to work due to health reasons. If they have a mortgage, there is a financial pressure for them to continue working. If they have paid off their mortgage, there is less financial pressure, and they may be able to stop or work less.

In 2022, more than 3.6 million people (27%) aged between 50 and 64 in the UK left the workforce due to the following reasons: 39% 'sick or disabled' because of stress, illness, mental health, and disability; 33% 'retired' because of redundancy, desire for lifestyle change, and job dissatisfaction; 14% 'looking after home or family' due to caring responsibilities; and 13% 'other' (ONS, 2022b). Evidence shows that those who choose to stop work early tend to be reasonably well-off. Of those who took early retirement in August 2022, for example, two-thirds (66%) own their homes without any outstanding mortgage and were debt free (61%) (ONS, 2022c). An absence of mortgage debt and financial pressure allows an individual to choose an option that is most appropriate for them.

### 3.2.11. Financial well-being

Having no debt and mortgage can confer individuals financial well-being, defined as a situation when a person is able to meet expenses and has some money left over, is in control of their finances, and feels financially secure, now and in the future (Salignac et al., 2020, p. 1596). Salignac et al. argue that financial well-being has three dimensions, shown in Figure 3.5.

Paying off a mortgage enables a homeowner to enjoy these three aspects of financial well-being:

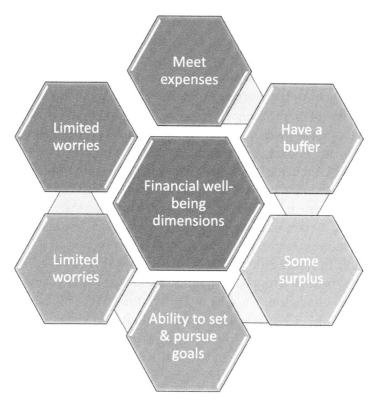

**Figure 3.5** *Dimensions of well-being*
*Source:* Adapted from Salignac et al., 2020

1) having eliminated the largest monthly expenditure, households will have more money to pay other expenses, build a buffer to meet the unexpected costs, and have money for life enjoyment;
2) they are in control over their financial situation now and the future, because their expenses are no longer affected by changes in interest rates and a lender's mortgage rate, and with more disposable income, they can set and pursue goals;
3) they will not have any financial worries regarding mortgage payments and so are likely to feel satisfied with their financial situation.

## 3.3. Disadvantages of paying off your mortgage early

### 3.3.1. Opportunity costs

Opportunity cost refers to the loss of potential benefits that may be received from alternative actions (e.g. investing). In the context of mortgage repayment, homeowners may miss out on possible returns if they allocate extra funds toward their mortgage rather than exploring other investment opportunities. Each mortgage payment essentially functions as a risk-free investment, as it reduces the homeowner's risk burden while providing a return equivalent to the mortgage's interest rate (e.g., a 1% mortgage rate yields a 1% return on the money). However, by focusing on early mortgage repayment, homeowners might overlook alternative investment options that offer greater returns. For instance, property investments, such as rental properties or commercial properties, can offer higher returns than mortgage interest rates and help diversify an investment portfolio. These investments can generate passive income and potentially appreciate over time.

The stock market has historically provided higher returns than most mortgage interest rates, and using surplus funds to pay off a mortgage could result in missing out on the long-term growth offered by stock market investments. This could significantly impact a homeowner's overall wealth accumulation. Since its inception, the FTSE 100 has averaged total returns of 7.75% per year – with an annualised return of 7.38% in the last ten years and 6.47% in the last 25 years (Bright, 2023). In contrast, average mortgage rates in the UK have ranged between 1–2.5% since 2009–2022. By using funds to pay off a mortgage instead of investing in periods of low interest rates, homeowners may potentially miss out on 4–5.5% returns on their money. However, interest rates have gone up substantially since, and the differential has reduced. With rates over 6%, investing is not as attractive as before.

Paying into a pension can be an appealing option, as individuals receive tax relief at 20%, 40%, or 45%. For example, a successful businessman who earns £200,000 per annum and pays 1% interest rate on his £400,000 mortgage. He has £35,000 surplus cash. His financial planner recommends him to use £35,000 to invest to generate a better return as his mortgage rate is only 1%, or contribute to his pension where he receives 45% tax relief. As an additional tax payer, he receives the highest tax relief (45%), and so a contribution of £35,000 will be grossed up to £63,636, representing an 82% return. However, he chooses to use the money to reduce his mortgage balance.

### 3.3.2. Personal sacrifices

Early mortgage repayment may require short-term sacrifices that could affect one's quality of life and well-being. Achieving this goal might entail cutting back on expenses like travelling, going on holiday, and dining out, and this may affect our well-being as we do not have an opportunity to relax, recharge, re-energise. It might also involve giving up financial objectives such as private education, which in turn might affect the academic performance of our children and their future. It may require taking on extra jobs to generate the necessary income for additional payments, and this reduces the amount of time we have to relax, sleep, and spend quality time with family and friends. In turn, this may exert stress on our personal relationships and marriage, resulting in elevated risk of social isolation, depression, and increased stress levels. Research also shows that working longer hours can increase the risk of heart disease, stroke, depression, alcoholism, neck, back, or chest pain, and type 2 diabetes.

### 3.3.3. Liquidity concerns

Liquidity refers to the ease with which homeowners can access their money. When homeowners pay off their entire debt, they lose liquidity, as they have exchanged cash for complete control of their property. In case of an emergency requiring funds, homeowners might need to remortgage (refinance) or sell the property to access the necessary money. Both methods can be time-consuming, and the ability to sell depends on various unpredictable factors such as market conditions, interest rates, supply and demand, and the buyer's situation. These factors could change by the time selling becomes necessary. If homeowners postpone paying off the mortgage and keep some cash in a savings account, they can access the money immediately when needed. Therefore, it is often recommended to only pay off the mortgage in full if there are sufficient funds set aside for emergencies.

One solution to the conflicting desire for liquidity and debt reduction is to use an offset mortgage. In an offset mortgage, homeowners set up a savings account linked to their mortgage, and interest earned on their savings is used to offset against the interest charged. Homeowners then only pay interest on the difference between the mortgage and the savings balance. For example, if the mortgage balance is £100,000 but homeowners have a savings balance of £20,000 in an offset savings account, interest is only charged on £80,000, as shown in Figure 3.6.

 MINUS  EQUAL

**Figure 3.6** *How an offset saving account works to reduce the mortgage chargeable balance*

Although the savings account is linked to a mortgage, homeowners can access the money at any time without affecting their mortgage. However, not all lenders offer this type of mortgage, and the interest rate on an offset mortgage is often higher.

### 3.3.4. Inflation and debt

Property ownership is often seen as a good tool to beat inflation for two reasons. First, property prices tend to follow inflation trends and so rise when prices increase. The relationship is not always positive, as property prices can fall due to changes in demand and supply, affordability, interest rates, and future expectations. However, as Michael Kitces points out, property ownership shields the owner from direct exposure to increased rent costs. In other words, owning a property (and using a mortgage to achieve ownership), instead of renting, allows homeowners to avoid rent inflation (which could be higher than price inflation) (Kitces, 2015).

Second, inflation reduces the value of mortgage debt and monthly mortgage payments because these are in nominal terms and do not increase in line with inflation. This means that rising inflation reduces the real value of mortgage debt and mortgage payments. A mortgage with a fixed interest rate can be used to beat inflation, because the *value* of the payment decreases over time due to inflation as the *amount* of the mortgage payment is the same every month.

Interest rates therefore need to be viewed in the context of inflation. If inflation is higher than interest rates, then the effective mortgage rate is negative, and positive when inflation is lower. As Table 3.2 shows, if inflation is 12% and mortgage rate is 11%, the effective mortgage rate is negative. If inflation is 5% and mortgage rate 6%, the effective mortgage rate is positive.

Table 3.2 *Mortgage and inflation*

| Mortgage rate | Inflation rate | Effective mortgage rate |
|---|---|---|
| 5% | 5% | 0% |
| 6% | 5% | 1% |
| 8% | 5% | 3% |
| 10% | 5% | 5% |
| 11% | 12% | −1% |
| 12% | 12% | 0% |

### 3.3.5. Effect on credit score

Paying off a mortgage is reported to have no significant effect on our credit score, partly because the amount of debt a person has is just one factor that affects credit score. However, it is possible that credit score may drop slightly after paying off a mortgage because of a reduction in credit mix (e.g. credit card, mortgage, car loan) and a fall in the average age of accounts an individual has (Akin, 2023).

### 3.4. Evaluating the choice between repayment or overpayment

In weighing up the decision to repay or overpay, it is worthwhile to consider this in a broader financial planning context by considering several factors:

a) **Emergency fund**: It is important to have an emergency fund to meet unexpected costs, and therefore setting up an emergency fund is considered a priority over making an extra contribution towards a mortgage.

b) **Debts**: If there are expensive, unsecured debts, it is generally recommended that these are paid off first before an overpayment on a mortgage is considered, because interest rates on unsecured debts tend to be higher.

c) **Protection**: Borrowers are recommended to consider three types of insurance to provide financial security. Adequate life insurance and critical illness cover are designed to provide a lump sum to pay off debts in the event of death and critical illness, while the purpose of income protection insurance is to ensure mortgage payments are paid in the event of long-term ill health.

d) **Pension contributions**: Pensions are a tax-efficient way to save because the government tops up your contributions with tax relief, and you might also receive employer contributions (depending on the scheme). As we live longer, we need to save more for retirement, and starting saving early is important to ensure contributions are affordable and that we can take advantage of compound interest.

e)  **Risk**: Which decision we take also depends on our attitude to risk – do we want to take risks in order to generate a higher return or do we want security? The other consideration is capacity for risk, which refers to the impact on our living standards if things do not work out. If you have a low attitude and capacity for risk, then a safer option is to save and overpay.

f)  **Penalties**: Some mortgage contracts charge their borrowers an early exit fee or an early redemption charge, in a bid to recoup some of the money they will lose in interest if the loan is repaid early. This is normally charged as a percentage of the loan and can be substantial. It is therefore important to check the terms and conditions of a mortgage contract before clearing a mortgage early or making a big lump sum payment because the cost of exit fees or penalty charges could outweigh the benefits. To avoid this, it might be necessary to wait until the date of early redemption charge expires or stay within the 10% overpayment limit allowed by lenders. This will be discussed in more detail in Chapter 5.

## 3.5. Conclusion

Whether to pay off a mortgage early is an individual choice, influenced by one's attitude towards debt and risk, financial situation, and mortgage rates. Those who are risk-averse may opt for the safer, guaranteed route of early mortgage repayment. Conversely, risk-tolerant borrowers might aim to maximise financial gains by investing surplus income for higher returns. However, this depends on the difference between mortgage rates and investment returns. The smaller the gap, the lower the incentive to invest.

In each scenario, it's assumed that individuals make conscious decisions, weigh up alternatives, and strategise for the future. However, in reality, borrowers might not fully comprehend available options or actively plan for repaying their largest debt. The following chapters outline the strategies you can adopt to optimise your mortgage.

# References

Akin, A. (2023). Should I pay off my mortgage early? *Experian*. Available at: www.experian.com/blogs/ask-experian/should-i-pay-off-my-mortgage-early/#:~:-text=No%2C%20paying%20off%20your%20mortgage,effect%20on%20your%20credit%20scores [Accessed 12 July 2023].

Ballentine, C., and Cachero, P. (2023). US homeowners are tapping $9 trillion in real estate wealth. *Bloomberg*, 15 July. Available at: www.bloomberg.com/news/articles/2023-07-15/rising-real-estate-prices-make-helocs-popular-for-owners-tapping-equity?leadSource=uverify%20wall [Accessed 16 July 2023].

Bankrate. (2023). Home equity data and statistics. Available at: www.bankrate.com/home-equity/homeowner-equity-data-and-statistics/ [Accessed 12 July 2023].

Bright, A. (2023). What are the average returns of the FTSE 100? *IG*. Available at: www.ig.com/uk/trading-strategies/what-are-the-average-returns-of-the-ftse-100–230511#:~:text=From%201984%20to%202022%2C%20the,a%20total%20return%20of%207.48%25.&text=How%20has%20FTSE%20100%20performed,10%20years%20(2012%20%E2%80%93%202022*)%3F [Accessed 12 July 2023].

Browning, S. (2023). Mortgage prisoners, House of Commons Library Research Briefing. Available at: https://researchbriefings.files.parliament.uk/documents/CBP-9411/CBP-9411.pdf [Accessed 7 October 2023].

City AM. (2023). Total UK housing wealth breaches £7 trillion for first time amid 'race for space'. *CityAM*. Available at: www.cityam.com/total-uk-housing-wealth-breaches-7-trillion-for-first-time-amid-race-for-space/ [Accessed 12 July 2023].

Corden, A., Hirst, M., and Nice, K. (2008). Financial implications of death of a partner. Available at: www.york.ac.uk/inst/spru/research/pdf/Bereavement.pdf [Accessed 12 July 2023].

Crawford, R. (2020). How does pension saving change when individuals complete repayment of their mortgage? Institute of Fiscal Studies Working Paper 20/39. Available at: https://ifs.org.uk/sites/default/files/output_url_files/WP202039-How-does-pension-saving-change-when-individuals-complete-repayment-of-their-mortgage.pdf [Accessed 8 June 2024].

English Housing Survey. (2021). English Housing Survey: Home ownership, 2019–20. Available at: https://assets.publishing.service.gov.uk/government/uploads/system/uploads/attachment_data/file/1000040/EHS_19-20_Home_ownership_report.pdf [Accessed 12 July 2023].

English Housing Survey. (2022). English Housing Survey 2021–2022: Headline report. Available at: www.gov.uk/government/statistics/english-housing-survey-2021-to-2022-headline-report/english-housing-survey-2021-to-2022-headline-report [Accessed 12 July 2023].

FCA. (2021). Mortgage prisoner review. Available at: www.fca.org.uk/news/news-stories/mortgage-prisoner-review [Accessed 7 October 2023].

Green, K. E. (2023). Mortgage prisoner trapped with bills £300 a month higher than his income after rates soar. *inews*. Available at: https://inews.co.uk/news/mortgage-prisoner-trapped-bills-300-a-month-higher-income-rates-soar-2532084 [Accessed 7 October 2023].

Hansen, S. (2022). Average home equity in the U.S. just hit a record high of $300,000. Available at: https://money.com/average-home-equity-record-high-3000000/#:~:text=According%20to%20a%20new%20report,still%20owe%20on%20your%20mortgage [Accessed 12 July 2023].

Kitces, M. (2015). Why a mortgage is not actually an inflation hedge itself, but can provide access to investments that are. Available at: www.kitces.com/blog/why-a-mortgage-is-not-actually-an-inflation-hedge-itself-but-can-provide-access-to-investments-that-are/ [Accessed 12 July 2023].

ONS. (2020). Living longer: Changes in housing tenure over time. Available at: www.ons.gov.uk/peoplepopulationandcommunity/birthsdeathsandmarriages/ageing/articles/livinglonger/changesinhousingtenureovertime [Accessed 12 July 2023].

ONS. (2022a). Household total wealth in Great Britain: April 2018 to March 2020. Available at: www.ons.gov.uk/peoplepopulationandcommunity/personalandhousehold finances/incomeandwealth/bulletins/totalwealthingreatbritain/april2018tomarch 2020 [Accessed 12 July 2023].

ONS. (2022b). Economic labour market status of individuals aged 50 and over, trends over time. Available at: www.gov.uk/government/statistics/economic-labour-market-status-of-individuals-aged-50-and-over-trends-over-time-september-2022/economic-labour-market-status-of-individuals-aged-50-and-over-trends-over-time-september-2022 [Accessed 12 July 2023].

ONS. (2022c). Reasons for workers aged over 50 years leaving employment since the start of the coronavirus pandemic: Wave 2. Available at: www.ons.gov.uk/employmentandlabourmarket/peopleinwork/employmentandemployeetypes/articles/reasonsforworkersagedover50yearsleavingemploymentsincethestart ofthecoronaviruspandemic/wave2 [Accessed 12 July 2023].

Prosser, D. (2023). How struggling Britons could unlock £7 trillion of property wealth. *Forbes*. Available at: www.forbes.com/sites/davidprosser/2023/03/30/how-struggling-britons-could-unlock-7-trillion-of-property-wealth/?sh=5ab74df426f3 [Accessed 12 July 2023].

Salignac, F., Hamilton, M., Noone, J., and Muir, K. (2020). Conceptualizing financial wellbeing: An ecological life-course approach. *Journal of Happiness Studies*. Available at: www.researchgate.net/publication/333950291_Conceptualizing_Financial_Wellbeing_An_Ecological_Life-Course_Approach [Accessed 12 July 2023].

Today's Conveyancer. (2021). Equity in UK homes reaches all-time high. *Today's Conveyancer*. Available at: https://todaysconveyancer.co.uk/equity-uk-homes-reaches-time-high/#:~:text=The%20report%20shows%20that%20London,East%20 Anglia%20at%20%C2%A3108%2C732 [Accessed 12 July 2023].

UK Mortgage Prisoners. (2023). Available at: www.ukmortgageprisoners.com/campaigns1 [Accessed 7 October 2023].

Wink, B., Lloyd, A., and Hoff, M. (2022). A mortgage now costs a third of the typical American income – the highest share since 2007. Available at: www.businessinsider.com/housing-market-homeowners-spending-third-of-income-mortgage-payments-2022-4?r=US&IR=T#:~:text=A%20mortgage%20payment%20on%20an,the%20end%20of%20last%20year [Accessed 12 July 2023].

# MASTERING MONEY MANAGEMENT SKILLS TO ACCELERATE MORTGAGE REPAYMENT AND ACHIEVE FINANCIAL FREEDOM

## 4.1. Introduction

Effective money management skills play a crucial role in achieving financial stability and independence. One of the primary goals for many individuals is to pay off their mortgage quicker, ultimately reducing interest payments and increasing home equity. By honing money management skills, homeowners can better allocate resources, budget wisely, and make informed financial decisions. This, in turn, can significantly impact the speed at which they repay their mortgage, allowing them to enjoy the benefits of a debt-free lifestyle sooner. This chapter will guide you through the process of cultivating money management skills and provide helpful tools to enhance the optimal use of your financial resources.

## 4.2. The single- and two-pronged approaches: the early mortgage payoff money management strategies

The early mortgage payoff strategy can be implemented using either a single- or two-pronged approach. The single-pronged approach emphasises cutting expenses, allowing the saved money to be used for mortgage overpayments. In contrast, the two-pronged approach involves not only reducing expenditures but also increasing income at the same time. This

DOI: 10.4324/9781003297765-4                                    49 dual method enables homeowners to allocate even more funds towards accelerating their mortgage repayment.

The single- and two-pronged approaches are directly associated with money management as they both require effective financial planning and resource allocation. In the single-pronged approach, an individual may analyse their monthly expenses, categorise them into essentials and non-essentials, identify non-essential spending where they can cut back (such as dining out), and focus on 'experiences over belongings'. By creating a strict spending budget and adhering to it, they can save money that can be used for additional mortgage payments. This strategy has helped many homeowners reduce the overall interest paid and shorten the mortgage term.

The two-pronged approach not only involves efficient expense management but also focuses on increasing income. A homeowner may decide to combine expense reduction with income generation. For example, they might rent out a room in their house, launch a side business, or invest in dividend-paying stocks. By simultaneously cutting costs and increasing income, they can allocate even more funds towards mortgage repayment. This approach has allowed numerous individuals to pay off their mortgages faster while also diversifying their financial portfolio.

Below are a few examples illustrating how homeowners can put the single- or two-pronged approach into practice. Once homeowners decide to prioritise mortgage repayment, their initial focus tends to be on reducing expenses, as this is an aspect within everyone's control. The key to managing expenses and living within one's means lies in effective budgeting. This process entails creating a budget and maintaining the discipline to adhere to the spending plan consistently.

- Elaine saves money by sticking to a spending budget and buying second-hand clothes. She increases her income by renting out a second bedroom and buying and fixing up properties. She pays off her mortgage in 12 years.
- Ian avoids spending on nice cars, jewellery, and trendy trainers. He chooses experiences over belongings. It takes him six years to pay off his mortgage, making him financially better off.
- Helen saves money by buying everything second-hand, borrowing or DIY, and sticking to a tight budget. She earns extra income through babysitting, puppy sitting, and working a second job as a receptionist. She pays off her mortgage in four years.

- Ali uses discount vouchers and swaps utility companies to save money. He increases his income by putting savings in high-interest accounts and using cashback sites. He pays off his mortgage in five years, allowing him to enjoy financial freedom and set up his own business.
- Eric and Emma sacrifice the latest gadgets, entertain friends by inviting them over for home-cooked meals rather than eating out, and focus on financial education. They remortgage to a cheaper deal when their loan to value (LTV) drops and take out an affordable mortgage based on a single income. It takes them seven years to pay off their mortgage.
- Alan saves money by avoiding nights out and not buying clothes. He increases his income by selling old computer games and investing cash in Premium Bonds.
- Ben receives money from cashback sites and uses this to overpay his mortgage.

## 4.2.1. Controlling spending tips

### 4.2.1.1 Budgeting

Creating a detailed monthly budget that outlines your income, fixed expenses, and variable expenses is essential for controlling spending. This could be done by reviewing two to three months of expenditure by going through bank and credit card statements to see where the money is being spent. We can then allocate an amount to each category of expenditure, including savings and discretionary spending, and track your daily expenses using a spreadsheet, mobile app, or pen and paper. This exercise will make us feel more empowered because it will help us identify our spending patterns and areas where we can cut back.

### 4.2.1.2 Careful use with credit card

Establishing short-term and long-term financial goals, such as paying off debt, building an emergency fund, or saving for a vacation, can motivate you to be more mindful of your spending habits. Limit your use of credit cards, which can encourage overspending, and opt for cash or debit cards for everyday purchases to make monitoring your spending easier. With many credit cards offering cashback, it can be tempting to play the system by doing day-to-day spending on them and letting the money accrue interest in the current account/savings. However, it is easy to build up a high credit card balance. Years ago, the author met a man in his early 30s who had several credit cards with a total balance of £120,000. This not only caused him a huge amount of stress but also affected his ability to get a mortgage.

### 4.2.1.3 Avoid impulsive spending

When shopping for groceries or other items, create a list beforehand, avoid going shopping on an empty stomach, and stick to the list to prevent impulse purchases and stay within your budget. Identify non-essential expenses (such as dining out, entertainment, and unused subscriptions), and find ways to reduce or eliminate them by cooking at home, finding free or low-cost entertainment options, or cancelling unused subscriptions. Before making a purchase, research prices and look for sales or discounts, and consider using price comparison websites or apps to ensure you're getting the best deal. To avoid impulse purchases, give yourself a 'reflective' period before making big-ticket or non-essential purchases, helping you determine if the item is truly necessary.

### 4.2.1.4 Pay off expensive debt

Focus on paying off high-interest debts, such as credit card balances, as they can significantly impact your financial health. Create a debt repayment plan and prioritise paying off the most expensive debt first, while paying the minimum amount on their other debts. Regularly review your budget and spending habits to identify areas of improvement, and make adjustments as needed to ensure you're staying on track to achieve your financial goals.

### 4.2.2. Increasing income tips

### 4.2.2.1 Salary increase

If you have been in your current job for a while and have consistently performed well, consider discussing a possible salary increase or promotion with your employer. Take advantage of opportunities to work overtime or take on additional projects if your job offers them, as this can help you earn extra income. Explore the job market to find positions that offer better compensation packages and be prepared to update your curriculum vitae (CV) and enhance your skills to make yourself more marketable.

### 4.2.2.2 Another income stream

Starting a part-time business or freelance work related to your skills or interests, such as graphic design, writing, photography, online tutoring, or consulting, can provide you with additional income and potentially grow into a full-time venture. Share your knowledge and expertise by teaching classes, workshops, or offering tutoring services in your area of expertise.

Start an online store or sell items on platforms like eBay, Etsy, or Amazon, which could include handmade crafts, vintage items, or products sourced from wholesalers. Finally, sign up for gig-based services such as Uber, Lyft, TaskRabbit, or Instacart to earn extra income during your spare time.

Consider renting out extra space in your home to generate more income.

### 4.2.2.3 Invest

Invest in income-generating assets, such as stocks that pay dividends, property, or peer-to-peer lending platforms, to create passive income streams.

### 4.2.2.4 Invest in yourself

Enhance your skill set and qualifications by pursuing higher education or industry-specific certifications, making you more valuable in the job market and increasing your earning potential. By exploring these options, you can increase your income and pay off your mortgage more quickly.

## 4.3. Personal financial plan

Managing your money well is essential for reaching your financial goals, both now and in the future. Good money management involves a variety of practices, such as planning for long-term goals, making smart spending choices, keeping a close eye on your finances, having contingencies in place to prepare for the unexpected, and staying in control of all aspects of your financial life. It also means using your limited resources wisely, being careful with your spending, and making the most of the money you have.

The key to successful money management is creating and sticking to a detailed personal financial plan. This plan acts as a guide, helping you work towards your financial goals and overcome any obstacles that might come up along the way. Research has shown that people who create and follow a financial plan tend to save more money, feel happier about their financial progress, and make better financial decisions, no matter how much money they make.

Creating a financial plan necessitates the execution of six key steps. Firstly, setting crystal clear goals is pivotal to defining your financial roadmap. Secondly, preparing a net worth statement gives you a snapshot of your financial standing and allows you to understand your assets and liabilities and net wealth. Thirdly, an income and expenditure statement is prepared to provide a comprehensive overview of your earnings and outflows, so that you can analyse your cash flow position and determine ways to improve it. The fourth step involves budgeting, which requires you to allocate your resources wisely to meet your financial needs and goals, setting up an emergency fund, buying an adequate level of insurance, and saving and investing. The fifth step is keeping accurate records and monitoring your financial progress, ensuring you stay on track. Lastly, regular reviews of your financial plan are essential to accommodate any changes in your financial situation or goals. Some people find the help of a financial planning professional valuable as an impartial thinking partner.

## 4.3.1. Goal setting

Goal setting is the foundation of success because it provides us with a roadmap, a sense of direction, discipline, and helps us to identify strategies and tools to achieve these and to stay focused. Goal clarity also leads to greater motivation to follow through with strategy, despite hardships. The more vivid and specific the goal, the better. Goals with a powerful 'why' attached work the best.

Short-term goals often include paying off debts, building an emergency fund, saving for a house deposit, and saving for travel. Long-term financial goals include paying off our mortgage, saving for retirement, and saving for a child's education.

Goal setting is a powerful process that helps you identify what you want to achieve and create a plan to reach those objectives. One effective method for setting goals is using the SMART framework, which stands for Specific, Measurable, Achievable, Relevant, and Time-bound. Additionally, incorporating visual elements into your goal-setting process can enhance motivation and make your goals more tangible.

- **Specific**: Clearly define your goal by writing down on a piece of paper exactly what you want to accomplish, and post it somewhere visible. This helps focus your efforts and provides a clear direction for your actions.
- **Measurable**: Establish criteria to track your progress and determine when you have achieved your goal. This may involve setting milestones or using quantifiable metrics.
- **Achievable**: Ensure that your goal is realistic and attainable given your current resources, skills, and constraints. This keeps you motivated and prevents feelings of frustration or disappointment.
- **Relevant**: Align your goal with your broader values, priorities, and long-term objectives. This ensures that your goal is meaningful and contributes to your overall growth and development.
- **Time-bound**: Set a deadline for achieving your goal to create a sense of urgency and encourage timely progress. This helps prevent procrastination and keeps you focused on your desired outcome.

## Visual Goal Setting:

- **Vision Board**: Create a collage of images, quotes, and affirmations that represent your goal. Display it in a prominent location to serve as a constant reminder and source of inspiration.
- **Mental Imagery**: Regularly visualise yourself achieving your goal, including the emotions, sensations, and experiences associated with success – what will it look like, be like to touch, sound like, smell like, and taste like. This can help build self-confidence, enhance motivation, and reinforce our commitment to our goal.
- **Progress Tracking**: Use visual aids, such as charts, graphs, or checklists, to monitor your progress towards your goal. Seeing your achievements can boost motivation and help you stay on track.

- **Goal Maps**: Break your goal down into smaller, actionable steps, and create a visual representation of the path to success. This can help clarify the process and make your goal feel more attainable.

Let's use the example of saving for a house deposit as a financial planning goal and apply both SMART and visual goal-setting techniques.

### SMART Goal:

Specific: Save £20,000 for a house deposit.

Measurable: Track your progress by monitoring your savings account balance and recording monthly contributions.

Achievable: Based on your current income and expenses, determine a realistic monthly saving amount that allows you to reach your goal without causing financial strain.

Relevant: This goal aligns with your long-term plan of homeownership and financial stability.

Time-bound: Set a deadline to save the £20,000 within three years.

### Visual Goal Setting:

- Vision Board: Create a vision board with images of your dream home, inspirational quotes about homeownership, and visual reminders of your £20,000 goal. Display it in a place where you'll see it daily to stay motivated.
- Mental Imagery: Regularly visualise yourself achieving your goal – signing the papers for your new house, receiving the keys, moving in, and the experiences you'll have in your new home. Imagine the sense of accomplishment and pride you'll feel when you reach your goal.
- Progress Tracking: Design a chart or graph to track your monthly savings contributions. Update it every month and celebrate your progress. Seeing the growth in your savings account visually can be highly motivating. When things do not go according to plan, look at the long-term progress, practice self-forgiveness, and try again.
- Goal Maps: Break down your goal into smaller, actionable steps. For example, create a timeline with milestones for each £1,000 saved. Visually map out these milestones along with any strategies you'll use to reach them, such as cutting expenses, increasing income, or investing.

By applying SMART and visual goal-setting techniques to your financial planning, you'll have a clear, achievable, and motivating goal to work towards.

## 4.4. Prepare a net worth statement

The next step in our financial plan is to establish our present situation by preparing a net worth statement (or balance sheet). A net worth statement adds up all our assets (things you own) and deducts from that our liabilities (things we owe). Knowing your net worth is important for several reasons:

- A solid starting point: A net worth statement helps you assess your current financial situation before creating any plans or setting goals. This baseline information allows you to identify areas for improvement and track your progress over time.
- Gauging financial health: Your net worth serves as a measure of your overall financial well-being. A positive net worth (assets > liabilities) indicates financial stability, while a negative net worth (assets < liabilities) suggests potential financial issues. Regularly reviewing your net worth statement helps you evaluate your financial health and make well-informed decisions.
- Spotting strengths and weaknesses: A net worth statement categorises your assets and liabilities (e.g., cash, investments, property, debts), giving you a detailed view of your finances. This helps you identify areas where you're doing well financially and those that may need attention or adjustments in your financial plan.
- Creating financial goals: Understanding your current net worth enables you to set realistic and meaningful financial objectives. For instance, you might aim to increase your net worth by a specific percentage within a certain timeframe or focus on reducing debt to improve your overall financial standing.
- Tracking progress: As you put your financial plan into action and modify your financial habits, regularly updating your net worth statement lets you monitor your progress and ensure you're on the right track. Comparing your net worth over time can be motivating and offer valuable insights into the effectiveness of your financial strategies.

To prepare a net worth statement, start by listing all your assets, which are the valuable items you own, see Table 4.1. Common asset categories include cash in current and savings accounts, investments such as stocks, bonds, and mutual funds, pensions, properties (primary residence and rental properties), personal property like vehicles, jewellery, and artwork, and any business ownership interests. For each asset category, determine its current market value by checking bank account balances, obtaining a property valuation, or estimating personal property values. Add up the values of all your assets to calculate your total assets.

Next, list all your liabilities, which are the debts and financial obligations you owe. Common liability categories include mortgages, secured debt and unsecured debt (car loans, credit card debt, personal loans, and overdraft). Determine the current outstanding balance for each liability category. Add up the amounts owed to calculate your total liabilities. Finally, to determine your net worth, subtract your total liabilities from your total assets: Net Worth = Total Assets − Total Liabilities. This calculation will provide you with an overall picture of your financial health.

## 4.5. Prepare an income and expenditure statement

Establishing a net worth statement is crucial, but it only provides a single perspective of our financial situation. To gain a more comprehensive understanding, it's essential to also analyse your cash flow position by preparing an income and expenditure statement. This will help you identify any surplus/deficit, and the key benefit is that you understand your financial situation better and can make more informed decisions about budgeting and financial planning.

This statement offers insights into the sources of our income and how we spend our money, as well as the amount of surplus income we have at our disposal, see Table 4.2. An income and expenditure statement involves listing all income sources, such as salary, investments, rental income, and any other revenues. Similarly, it requires documenting all expenses, including housing costs, utility bills, groceries, transportation, debt repayments, and discretionary spending. By comparing the total income and total expenses, we can determine our surplus or deficit cash flow.

Our spending is likely to vary over the year, and so creating a monthly income and expenditure statement helps us identify the times of year when our spending is at its highest (for example, during summer vacations or the holiday season) and when it's at its lowest. It's essential to categorise our expenses as either essential or non-essential. This way, we can understand the minimum income we need to cover our basic needs and identify areas where we can reduce spending.

**Table 4.1** *How to prepare a net worth statement*

| | £ |
|---|---|
| Networth statement for | |
| | |
| Date prepared | |
| | |
| **ASSETS** | |
| *Personal assets* | |
| House (main residence) | |
| Car | |
| Contents | |
| **Total personal assets** | |
| | |
| *Cash/liquid assets* | |
| Cash in bank account 1 | |
| Cash in bank account 2 | |
| Other liquid assets | |
| **Total value of cash/liquid assets** | |
| | |
| *Investments* | |
| Investment 1 | |
| Investment 2 | |
| Investment 3 | |
| | |
| **Total value of investments** | |
| | |
| *Pensions* | |
| Pension fund 1 | |
| Pension fund 2 | |
| **Total value of pensions** | |
| | |
| **LIABILITIES** | |
| Mortgage outstanding | |
| Loans | |
| Overdraft | |
| Credit card | |
| Other borrowings | |
| **Total liabilities** | |
| | |
| **Networth (assets minus liabilities)** | |

*Note:* To complete the table, fill in the values in the relevant boxes. Add up your assets. Add up your liabilities. Take your total liabilities away from your total assets to work out your net worth.

**Table 4.2** *How to prepare an income and expenditure statement*

| Income and expenditure statement (state tax year) | | |
|---|---|---|
| | *Annual (£)* | *Monthly (£)* |
| **INCOME** | | |
| | | |
| Salary | | |
| Rental income | | |
| Interest | | |
| Dividend | | |
| Other income (e.g. benefits) | | |
| Total gross income | | |
| Less tax | | |
| **Total household net income per annum** | | |
| **Total household net income per month** | | |
| | | |
| **EXPENDITURE** | | |
| | | |
| Mortgage | | |
| Utilities | | |
| Housekeeping | | |
| Motor | | |
| Travel and Leisure | | |
| Personal spending | | |
| Insurance | | |
| Savings/investments | | |
| Pension contributions | | |
| **Total Spending per annum** | | |
| **Total Spending per month** | | |
| | | |
| **Total annual surplus** | | |
| **Total monthly surplus** | | |

*Note:* To complete the table, fill in the values for each income and expense category. Then, add up the income. Add up your expenses. Take away your total expenses from your total income to identify whether you have a surplus or a deficit.

Additionally, it's crucial that you treat saving as a top priority instead of an optional goal. By adopting the 'pay yourself first' approach, we set aside a portion of our income for saving before allocating funds to other expenses. This mindset encourages financial discipline and ensures we are consistently working toward building our financial security.

## 4.6. Prepare a budget

Budgeting is critical to money management, and its aim is to enable us to balance our income and spending and ensure that we do not spend more money than we receive. It therefore helps us avoid debt and live within our means. It also assists us take control of our finance and gives us the power to shape our future because preparing a budget involves thinking ahead and planning expenditure in advance and setting limits to our expenditure (by allocating a specific amount/percentage to each category of expenses). This makes us become more conscious of our spending and where our money goes as well as more critical of the way we spend money.

Creating a budget involves five steps, see Table 4.3:

a)  **Estimate income**: The first step is to estimate the total amount of income we receive for a given period – this could be daily, weekly, monthly, and annually. A monthly budget appears to be most common as many people get paid on this basis. However, income has to be take-home pay, that is, the amount we have left to spend after taking off taxes and other deductions (e.g. salary sacrifice for pension, healthcare, bike, car).

b)  **Estimate spending**: The second step is to estimate spending, including mortgage/rent, food, council tax, utilities, travel, insurance, discretionary spending. Many companies bill us on a monthly basis, and so working on a monthly basis might be easier.

c)  **Budget saving**: Many people find it difficult to save. A common mistake is to wait until the end of the month and see what is left before saving. Often this means that there is nothing left to save. To ensure that money is set aside, we need to pay ourselves first. This involves putting aside a sum or percentage of money before spending. This is known as 'paying yourself first' and goes before expenditure.

**Table 4.3** *How to prepare a budget*

| | January | February | March | April | May | June | July | August | September | October | November | December |
|---|---|---|---|---|---|---|---|---|---|---|---|---|
| **INCOME** | | | | | | | | | | | | |
| Salary | | | | | | | | | | | | |
| Bonus/overtime | | | | | | | | | | | | |
| Income from savings/ investments | | | | | | | | | | | | |
| Benefits | | | | | | | | | | | | |
| | | | | | | | | | | | | |
| Total income | | | | | | | | | | | | |
| **EXPENDITURE** | | | | | | | | | | | | |
| Mortgage | | | | | | | | | | | | |
| Utilities | | | | | | | | | | | | |
| Housekeeping | | | | | | | | | | | | |
| Motor | | | | | | | | | | | | |
| Travel and Leisure | | | | | | | | | | | | |
| Personal spending | | | | | | | | | | | | |
| Insurance | | | | | | | | | | | | |
| Savings/investments | | | | | | | | | | | | |
| Pension contributions | | | | | | | | | | | | |
| **SURPLUS/DEFICIT** | | | | | | | | | | | | |

d) **Budget fixed, variable, and discretionary expenses**: We need to assign an amount to each category of expenditure such as fixed (e.g. mortgage), variable (e.g. food, energy, petrol) and discretionary (e.g. eating out, holidays). This helps us understand the minimum amount of money we need to live.

e) **Establish shortfall or surplus**: After doing a budget, we will be able to see if we have a surplus or deficit. If there is a deficit, it is important to review all expenses and see what can be cut. Mortgage costs are usually the largest expense, and there may be scope to reduce costs by changing to a better deal. Spending on food can also be cut by shopping at discount stores or substituting products for lesser-known brands. To ensure a surplus, it might be prudent to underestimate income and overestimate your spending in a budget.

It is often suggested that families may face financial difficulties if they allocate more than 20% of their income towards debt repayment. This could lead to potential challenges in managing other expenses and achieving financial stability. We can calculate the percentage of income spent on debt payments by adding together all the debt payments (including mortgages) and dividing by our net annual income. For example: all debt payments for 12 months is £10,000 and net annual income is £30,000, giving the percentage spent on debt payments of 30%. Reducing debt or increasing income, or both, lowers the percentage spent on debt payments. It is recommended that families should not spend more than 20–30% of their income on debt repayment.

## 4.7. Keep records of spending and saving

The fifth step in managing personal finances is to consistently track and document our spending and saving habits. By maintaining accurate records of our financial transactions, we can gain a clearer understanding of our cash flow and ensure that we're adhering to our budget. To achieve this, update the actual column of your income and expenditure statement on a weekly basis. This process allows you to compare your actual spending and saving with the budgeted amounts, helping you identify any discrepancies or areas where adjustments may be necessary. Regularly monitoring your financial activity also encourages financial discipline and accountability, making it easier to stay on track with your financial goals.

## 4.8. Review your plan

It's crucial to regularly review and assess your financial plan to ensure you're making progress towards your financial goals. By evaluating your plan consistently, you can identify any changes in your financial situation, such as fluctuations in income, unexpected expenses, or shifts in your priorities.

When reviewing your financial plan, it's essential to review the following areas:

- **Spending**: Compare your actual spending and saving patterns with the budgeted amounts, identifying any discrepancies or areas that may need adjustments.
- **Investments**: Analyse your investment portfolio (e.g. level of risk, asset allocation) and its performance, determining if any adjustments are required, such as rebalancing your asset allocation or diversifying your investments.
- **Progress**: Assess your progress towards both short-term and long-term financial objectives, such as building an emergency fund, paying off debt, or saving for retirement.
- **Goals**: Revisit your financial goals, ensuring they remain relevant and achievable while making any necessary modifications to align with your current situation or aspirations.

These steps will help you maintain a comprehensive and up-to-date financial plan that serves your needs and goals effectively.

## 4.9. Apps to help with money management

Technology has made it easier to manage our money and help you repay your mortgage quicker. In choosing a suitable app to use, it is worth to bear a few points in mind:

- **FCA regulation**: Check to see if it is regulated by the Financial Conduct Authority (FCA) as this offers you consumer protection.
- **Depositor protection schemes** (FSCS): Check to see if it is covered by the Financial Services Compensation Scheme as this will protect your money.

- **Good reputation**: Check the reputation of the company which develops the app, and don't just look at the positive reviews.
- **Fees**: Apps may not charge a fee, and you may pay for them with your personal data (e.g. what products you buy).

**Budgeting**: Some apps help you manage your money by using artificial intelligence to analyse your monthly spending, calculate how much you can afford to save each month, and suggest where spending can be cut. They can also automatically transfer money into a savings account to earn interest and feed a weekly flow of cash back to the everyday account to cover spending.

**Cashback apps**: Some apps work as a cashback app, rewarding you with money back when you spend at any of their retail partners. The cashback you earn accumulates in your account on your app, and once the balance reaches a certain level, the money can be paid directly to your mortgage lender.

**Rounding up apps**: Some apps round up purchases you make on your card to the nearest pound and put the spare change in an account which you could then use to overpay your mortgage payments. They may also offer accounts to help you save for a house purchase or retirement planning.

**Money management apps**: Some apps offer several facilities to help you manage your money, including the following:
  - Budgeting: Some apps leverage the power of Open Banking to link all your banking accounts in one place and help you budget by planning your monthly expenditure, identifying wasteful subscriptions, and calculating how much you can afford to commit to mortgage overpayments. However, we should be careful who we give the permission to access our bank accounts.
  - Investing: Some apps offer the facility to trade and invest as little as £1.
  - Payments: Send and request money by sending payment links or flashing QR codes.
  - Saving: Offers an easy-access savings account.
  - Borrowing: You can borrow money for a car, home improvements, or debt consolidation.

In summary, there are many technologies to help you manage your money, but they should be used with great caution to avoid scams.

## 4.10. Conclusion

Effective money management skills are crucial for achieving financial stability and successfully navigating the complexities of mortgages and other financial commitments. By setting realistic goals, diligently tracking expenses, and regularly reviewing your financial plan, you can make informed decisions that lead to long-term financial success.

A well-structured budget and a strong understanding of your financial situation will not only help you manage your mortgage payments but also enable you to adapt to any changes in your circumstances.

Ultimately, mastering money management skills empowers you to take control of your financial future, ensuring that you can confidently face any challenges and seize opportunities that come your way.

CHAPTER FIVE

OPTIMISING MORTGAGE MANAGEMENT STRATEGIES

## 5.1. Introduction

Monthly mortgage payments are often the largest household expense, and this financial commitment is carried over a great part of our working life. Paying off our mortgage early enables us to significantly reduce our monthly outgoings and save thousands of pounds of interest. In addition, we'll feel relieved and enjoy peace of mind and higher financial well-being. Yet, paying off a mortgage prematurely is regarded a lofty aspiration and may overstretch a household finance. This chapter discusses how an effective mortgage management strategy reduces costs and outlines strategies to pay off your mortgage early.

## 5.2. Affordable mortgage

Before we buy a property, we have to make many mortgage-related decisions. We need to establish the price brackets of the property we can afford and the level of deposit we can or wish to put down. Some buyers want to buy a property at the higher range, put down a small deposit, and borrow the maximum amount offered by the lender; while others want to buy a property at a lower price range, put down a bigger deposit, and choose a smaller mortgage than the one they are offered.

DOI: 10.4324/9781003297765-5

Richard and Sian, for example, could borrow £190,000 from the bank, and with a 15% deposit, they could buy a property in the region of £223,000. However, they did not wish to borrow the maximum because they wanted to ensure that their mortgage payment and essential bills were affordable on one wage. They therefore saved £35,000 for a deposit in six years, chose a cheaper property costing £112,500, and borrowed £95,000 instead (they kept some money for renovation). In addition to getting a smaller mortgage loan, they also overpaid £160 per month (41% on top of monthly mortgage payments of £394) and this enabled them to pay off their mortgage in seven years, or 28 years early. This allows them to enjoy a mortgage-free lifestyle, conferring a 'priceless' sense of freedom.

## 5.3. Ways to repay a mortgage

### 5.3.1. Repayment mortgage

There are two ways to repay a mortgage: a repayment mortgage and interest only. Choosing a repayment mortgage is important because it is a guaranteed way for us to repay a mortgage at the end of the term. Each monthly mortgage payment is allocated in two ways:

- A portion goes to pay the simple interest on outstanding debt
- The remainder goes to repay a portion of the loan or amount borrowed

It is a risk-free, straightforward, and guaranteed method to repay the mortgage. It is also a contractual form of saving because the lender works out how much we need to pay monthly, based on the interest rate and term of the mortgage chosen, and the payment is taken automatically via a direct debit. In early years of a mortgage, a large part of the monthly payment is made up of the interest element, but as the years progress, a greater proportion goes towards the repayment of the loan.

As the amount of outstanding debt is reduced, the portion of the payment to pay interest decreases while the part devoted to the loan increases. It takes many years of monthly payments to significantly reduce the outstanding balance of the loan. As the loan is slowly being repaid, the homeowner builds up gradually their equity. This represents the amount that has been paid off plus any appreciation in the value of the property.

## 5.3.2. Interest-only mortgage

With an interest-only mortgage, the mortgage debt remains the same throughout the term, as we have not repaid any of the capital borrowed. Although this makes monthly payment more affordable, we still have to find a way to repay the debt at the end of the term. For example, if we take out a mortgage for £100,000 over 25 years on an interest-only mortgage, we still owe £100,000 at the end of 25 years because we have only paid the interest on the loan and not the capital borrowed (e.g. the mortgage loan of £100,000). If we go for a repayment mortgage, we will have repaid all the loan after 25 years and owe the house outright.

There are several reasons why some borrowers might opt for an interest-only mortgage. Firstly, the monthly payment is lower than the monthly payment on a repayment mortgage because we do not pay off the amount we borrow. This might be attractive to borrowers who expect their financial situation to improve (e.g. through promotion, inheritance). The salary of professionals such as doctors, dentists, solicitors normally rises after they complete their training, and so an interest-only mortgage is used as a temporary measure to manage their cashflow.

Secondly, interest-only mortgages are a popular option for investment properties that are rented out. In this scenario, the property owner does not reside in the property, allowing them to potentially sell the property at the end of the mortgage term to repay the loan. This approach can provide several benefits for property investors, such as lower monthly payments and increased cash flow, as they are only required to pay the interest portion of the mortgage during the term. Additionally, it allows investors to focus on maximising rental income and property appreciation, which can contribute to higher returns on their investment. By strategically utilising an interest-only mortgage for rental properties, investors can take advantage of these benefits while still ensuring they have a plan in place to repay the loan at the end of the term.

Thirdly, some borrowers might opt for an interest-only mortgage because they might be able to get a better return by investing the difference in monthly payments. A monthly payment on a repayment mortgage is higher than an interest-only mortgage monthly payment. By investing the difference in monthly payments in investment vehicles such as ISAs, borrowers can accumulate a lump sum to repay the mortgage. This is a riskier method and does not guarantee that the mortgage will be paid off at the end of the term.

Since the financial crisis, lenders have become stricter and require borrowers to repay both capital and interest on residential mortgages (those for owners to live in). The English Housing Survey found that 98% of first-time buyers have a repayment mortgage in 2021–2022. Interest-only mortgages are only permitted in special circumstances, such as those who can prove that they have other assets (e.g. equity from other properties) which they can use to repay the loan at the end of the mortgage term.

## 5.4. Choice of mortgage

The type of mortgage we choose also influences how soon we can repay a mortgage. There are several types of mortgages: fixed-rate, tracker, discounted, variable rate, and offset mortgages. We will now discuss the pros and cons of each type.

### 5.4.1. Fixed-rate mortgages

A fixed-rate mortgage is often attractive as it offers certainty and security. As the interest rate chosen does not change during the fixed period, a fixed-rate mortgage makes it easier to budget as borrowers know how much their monthly mortgage payments are. Fixed rates are therefore popular. According to the Bank of England, mortgages with long-term fixed rates (five years or more) accounted for half of new mortgage lending in the UK in 2019 Q4 (Bank of England, 2020).

The main disadvantages of a fixed-rate mortgage are that interest rates can be higher than other types of mortgages, and they often have an early redemption penalty (e.g. a fine for changing, moving, or repaying the mortgage early, or overpaying by more than 10%). This is often charged as a percentage of the amount borrowed, and the penalty can be substantial. For example, if you have a £100,000 mortgage with 3% early redemption charge (known as ERC), then you will need to pay £3,000 if you repay the mortgage. Penalty might be charged as a flat rate (e.g. 3% if you repay at any time during the fixed period) or descending scale (e.g. 3% in year 1, 2% in year 2, and 1% in year 3). A fixed-rate mortgage therefore is less flexible and does not easily accommodate a change in personal circumstance (e.g. a new job in a different location, or a sale of the family home in divorce).

We need to choose a mortgage with special care, as getting out of this type of deal can be extremely expensive. Years ago, we met a lady who had a fixed-rate mortgage and had to pay a £28,000 penalty because she needed to move her mortgage to another lender to raise money on her property to fund other goals (e.g. set up a business). A fixed-rate mortgage is premised on stability in terms of income, employment, and personal circumstances, and a change in any of these (loss of income, loss of employment, and a relationship breakdown) can prove expensive.

### 5.4.2. Tracker mortgages

A tracker-rate mortgage is a mortgage with an interest rate normally linked to the Bank of England base rate. A lender often charges a loading on top of the Bank of England (BoE) base rate (e.g. 0.5% + BoE base rate), and the interest rate will move in line with changes in the base rate. This type of mortgage is particularly attractive when rates are expected to fall. Lenders can offer tracker-rate mortgages with or without early redemption penalties. Taking out a tracker-rate mortgage with no early redemption penalty gives you the freedom to switch to a fixed-rate mortgage when rates are expected to rise.

There are two types of trackers: a lifetime tracker (tracks for the life of the mortgage) and a term tracker (for a fixed number of years, e.g. two to three years). In a stable interest rate environment, a lifetime tracker means you do not need to keep changing deals every few years and paying product fees. A term tracker, on the other hand, often involves you switching to another deal and paying a product fee.

### 5.4.3. Discounted mortgages

Lenders also offer discounted mortgages. These are mortgages which enjoy a discount off the lender's variable rate for a fixed period of time, and again many of them have an early redemption penalty. Once your initial deal ends, you may need to change your deal (and pay a fee to the lender to change).

### 5.4.4. Variable rate mortgages

A standard variable rate mortgage offers you the most flexibility as they do not often have an early redemption penalty. In other words, borrowers can change, move, or pay off their mortgage at any time without paying a penalty. For this flexibility, you often have to pay an interest rate which is higher than other deals available.

Variable rate mortgages are different from tracker mortgages because the rates are determined by the lender and are not linked to the Bank of England's base rate. Although they can offer more flexibility, variable rate mortgages offer less certainty because the criteria to determine future rates are unknown.

Many borrowers do not start out with a variable mortgage but lapse to the standard variable rate after an initial deal ends, often without realising it or knowing that they have a better alternative. Research shows that 46% of mortgage holders are unaware that they can move to a new deal when a current deal expires, partly due to a lack of understanding (some homeowners are confused by the term remortgaging, believing it involves taking on more debt or a second mortgage, or have a limited understanding of the meaning of a standard variable rate mortgage) while others fail to act due to fear (that lenders might scrutinise their finances in times of economic uncertainty). As a result, a quarter of mortgage holders 'needlessly' lose money every month by paying the variable rate, or the maximum interest charged by a lender, costing them as much as £4,080 of additional interest each year (Green, 2022). If you wish to save money on your mortgage, it is advisable to avoid variable rates (unless there are special reasons – e.g. waiting for an inheritance so that you can pay off a large chunk of your mortgage).

According to the Institute of Fiscal Studies, over the period 2018–2020, 30% of mortgage holders had a variable rate mortgage. They represent 10% of the population or 7 million people. A higher proportion of variable rate holders fall into older and low-income households – 36% in the lowest-income fifth of the population and 44% in the age group 55–59 (Cribb and Sturrock, 2022). It appears that the most vulnerable groups in society are most exposed to mortgage rate rise risk.

Research commissioned by the FCA into the reasons why people do not change their mortgage shows that there are three key barriers:

a)   Non-switchers are content with their mortgage deal, and many are loyal to their current lender.
b)   They overestimate the difficulties of switching and find the process overwhelming, particularly considering the various mortgage options, lenders, associated fees, and terms. They also lead busy lives, including full-time jobs, children, and hobbies, and have a limited capacity and time to engage with the process.

c)   They underestimate the benefits of doing so: many non-switchers are unconvinced that they would be able to save a significant amount of money through switching their mortgage, either because they feel they are already on a good deal or because they feel that the savings would be offset by various fees. Indeed, the complexity of the product helps to contribute to the uncertainty around how much they would save (FCA, 2020, p. 56).

However, some households, known as 'mortgage prisoners', are unable to switch to a better deal due to stringent lending criteria introduced after the financial crisis, as discussed in Chapter 2 (Browning, 2023, p. 5).

### 5.4.5. Offset mortgages

Offset mortgages are less popular than other types of mortgages and are designed to allow you to offset savings against borrowings. You might have a savings and a mortgage account with the same lender. In other words, you might save and borrow at the same time. An offset mortgage allows you to pay interest only on the net amount borrowed, as lenders deduct the amount of savings from the mortgage balance and charge interest on the difference. For example, you might borrow £100,000 from a lender but might have £5,000 in a savings account with the same bank. Having an offset mortgage means that you only pay interest on the differential amount (£95,000). This can help homeowners potentially reduce their mortgage term and save thousands in interest. This is especially beneficial for higher (40%) and additional rate tax-payers (45%) who would potentially have paid income tax at 40%/45% on the savings interest. By putting savings in an offset account, borrowers potentially put the tax into their mortgage instead of paying the HMRC.

Offset mortgages were popular in the late 1990s and early 2000s, but since then they have fallen out of favour. However, offset mortgages appear to be becoming popular again, partly due to the financial side effects of the pandemic, when some consumers have been able to build up large pots of 'lockdown savings'. They may earmark a sum of money for home improvements projects or buying another property, but they do not know when, or even if, this will happen, and in the meantime their money is not earning any interest in a bank account. They therefore want to make their money work harder by putting it in an offset account. This offers them accessibility (can access their money anytime), higher returns (bank savings rates have been poor), and security of their capital (in comparison to investing in the stock market). Indeed, Ray Boulger, a leading mortgage broker, points out that the beauty of an offset mortgage is that it is the only type of mortgage that allows the homeowner to reborrow any overpayments without subjecting to an affordability check. This is because you are not technically borrowing more money but simply withdrawing funds from your savings account (Jones, 2021).

An offset mortgage is attractive in several ways. Firstly, it is tax efficient because you do not earn any interest on your savings as you offset this against the cost of your mortgage and therefore do not pay any tax on the interest earned. This is particularly good for higher-rate taxpayers. Secondly, you effectively receive the same rate of interest on your savings as you pay on your mortgage. Often lenders charge a higher interest rate on mortgages and pay a lower interest rate on savings. In an offset mortgage, the amount of savings is deducted from the mortgage loan, and so in effect borrowers receive the same interest rate on their savings as they pay on their mortgage. Although an offset mortgage can potentially help you pay off the loan quickly and save you money, few lenders offer offset mortgages, and these tend to be more expensive than standard mortgages.

**Table 5.1** *Pros and cons of various mortgage options*

| Types of mortgage | Advantages | Disadvantages |
|---|---|---|
| **Tracker** | Transparency if linked to Bank of England base rate<br>Benefit from rate reductions if rates fall | No certainty as rates can go up |
| **Discounted** | Discounts on interest rate | Early redemption penalty |
| **Variable** | Flexibility and freedom to move your mortgage | Rates tend to be higher than other deals |
| **Fixed** | Certainty<br>Makes budgeting easier<br>Protection against interest rate rises | Early redemption penalty<br>No flexibility during fixed period |
| **Offset** | Reduce term of mortgage<br>Tax efficiency<br>Interest rate on savings same as mortgage | Rates might be higher<br>Limited choice of lenders<br>Need to have savings |

## 5.5. Save product fees

Many mortgage deals in the UK tend to be two, three, and five years, and a few fixed rate mortgage deals for ten years. Whether you should go for a two-, three-, five- or ten-year deal depends on many considerations, including:

- Your future plans: How long do you plan to live in the property? Are you likely to move to a bigger property in a few years? How likely are you to move jobs and place of work in the future?
- Affordability: which deal is more affordable?
- Fees: what are the fees associated with different deals? What is the early redemption charge?
- Outlook on mortgage rates: what is the expectation of future interest rates? Are they on rising or falling?

In a low interest rate environment, two- to three-year deals might be cheaper than a longer term deal and gives you more flexibility if you wish to pay more than the 10% facility (most mortgages offer borrowers the chance to overpay by 10% of the loan per year). However, when the deal ends, you will have to move to another product, and a more competitive deal often involves paying another product fee.

In a rising interest rate environment, a longer-term deal (five, ten years) gives you more security and saves you product fees, as you do not need to keep taking out a new product and pay a fee within this period. However, it offers less flexibility if there is a change in your requirements and circumstances.

## 5.6. Switch to a cheaper deal

Since the financial crisis in 2007–2008, many lenders price the interest rate on loan to value (e.g. outstanding debt in relation to property value). Properties with a high loan to value represent a higher risk (e.g. risk of missing payments/defaulting, risk of the property becoming less valuable than the amount outstanding), and so lenders charge a higher rate to reflect this.

However, after a period of time, your loan to value should reduce, allowing you to switch to a cheaper deal (providing there is no penalty to do so). There are two possible reasons why the loan to value decreases with time. First, if you have a repayment mortgage, you would have paid off some capital owned, and this reduces your debt and lowers your loan to value. A couple bought their three-bedroom semi-detached house for £130,000, and overpayments on their repayment mortgage led to a significant drop in their loan-to-value ratio from 85% to 60% within two years. This not only accelerated their path to becoming debt-free but also opened up access to more advantageous deals (Otter, 2021).

Lee and Clare succeeded in paying off their £160,000 mortgage 28 years ahead of schedule by meticulously saving and making regular overpayments. The couple purchased their home with an initial mortgage term set for 35 years. Nevertheless, they devised a savings plan that facilitated consistent overpayments on their mortgage. As a result, their loan-to-value ratio dropped from 83% to 50% within just four years. This significant decrease enabled them to switch to a more cost-effective deal. To achieve this, they simply contacted their lender at the end of their initial deal to request offers based on their new loan-to-value ratio.

Second, changes in property prices also affect the loan to value, reducing the loan to value in a rising market and increasing it in a falling market. For example, David buys a house for £150,000 with a loan of £135,000. A few years later, the value of the house increases to £200,000, and so his loan to value falls from 90% to 67.5%, allowing him to access more preferential deals. However, if the property value falls to £140,000, the loan to value increases to more than 96%.

## 5.7. How to pay off a mortgage quickly?

The preceding section delved into various strategies for reducing mortgage costs and managing your home loan more effectively. Now, we will transition into exploring methods to accelerate your mortgage repayment timeline. This section aims to equip you with an array of tactics that can help you pay off your mortgage at a faster rate, thereby freeing you from debt sooner than expected. From making overpayments to restructuring your mortgage plan, there are multiple avenues you can consider to expedite your journey towards a mortgage-free life. Let's examine these strategies in detail.

### 5.7.1. Shorten the term

One way to pay off a mortgage quickly is to shorten the term of the mortgage. The shorter the period you borrow, the less interest you pay and the quicker you can pay off your mortgage. Many of us are programmed to regard a 25-year mortgage term as the norm. However, we do not need to take this long to pay off our mortgage if we can afford to do so over a shorter period. Changing this mindset can help us speed up the process of paying off our debt.

Years ago, a couple bought a three-bed house and rented out two rooms and used the money to overpay the mortgage. They also had no children and worked at weekends and evenings to earn extra money to overpay the mortgage. They managed to pay off the mortgage in a few years, instead of the usual 25-year timescale. This involved a lot of personal sacrifice and hard work in the short term, but it meant that they were able to enjoy a life without a mortgage early in life before the arrival of their children.

However, high property prices mean that many borrowers have to borrow over a longer period of time to make monthly payments affordable. Borrowers traditionally have gone for a 25-year mortgage, but lenders increasingly offer a maximum term of 40 years. The English Housing Survey shows that of those first-time buyers who took out a mortgage in 2021–2022, 56% opted for a repayment term of more than 30 years, 38% for a term between 20 and 29 years, and only a small percentage (6%) went for a shorter term of one to 19 years. In comparison to 2021–2021, the percentage of first-time buyers taking out a mortgage with a 30-year or longer term has reduced.

Although the main advantage of spreading the loan over a longer period of time is a lower monthly payment and greater affordability, homeowners desire to pay off the loan more quickly (i.e. a shorter repayment term) for several reasons. Firstly, the total interest paid will be lower. Shorter-term repayment also has other advantages, including a faster build-up of equity in the property and a forced method of saving. After the debt is paid off, we can enjoy a feeling of financial security and

Table 5.2 *Growing popularity of longer-term mortgages*

| Term of mortgage | 2019–2020 | 2020–2021 | 2021–2022 |
|---|---|---|---|
| **30 years or more** | 45% | 62% | 56% |
| **20–29 years** | 49% | 33% | 38% |
| **1–19 years** | 6% | 5% | 6% |

Source: English Housing Survey (EHS), 2019–20 (pp. 12–3), 2020–21 (p. 16) and 2021–22

freedom as a result of having no mortgage. However, a shorter term can result in a high monthly mortgage payment and put individuals under financial pressure. A better solution is to opt for a longer repayment period and overpay to pay off the loan early. This reduces financial pressure and makes faster payoff optional rather than mandatory.

### 5.7.2. Off-setting

A second way to pay off a mortgage quickly is to offset the costs of borrowing against the interest you earn on your savings. An offset mortgage works by allowing you to offset the cost of interest paid on the mortgage account against the interest earned on your saving account. The additional benefit is you receive the same level of interest on savings as the rate they pay on your mortgage.

### 5.7.3. Overpayment

A third method is to pay more than the required monthly amount. Homeowners might receive a lump sum as a bonus or inheritance. Keith receives a £5,000 bonus from work and uses this to overpay his mortgage.

Any overpayment can help you reduce the period you borrow money and save you interest. Most lenders allow borrowers to overpay by 10% of the balance of the mortgage every year. If you borrow £100,000, for example, a lender allows you to pay back 10% (£10,000) per year even if a mortgage has an early redemption penalty. If you overpay 10% every year, this means that you can repay your mortgage in less than ten years.

Instead of paying off a lump sum, you can also overpay an extra amount every month (within the 10% limit per annum). Let's assume that you have a mortgage with a balance of £100,000, you pay interest rate of 5%, and you borrow over a 25-year term. If you overpay £100 per month, you'll pay off your mortgage six years and two months earlier (see Money Saving Expert calculator).

## 5.8. Extra tactics to accelerate your mortgage repayment

### 5.8.1. Live on one income, and use the other to pay your mortgage

In some countries, it is recommended that households with two incomes can accelerate their mortgage repayment by living on one income and using the other income to pay off the mortgage. A couple might be accustomed to living on both of their incomes. Rather than living on both incomes, they can increase their savings and pay off their mortgage quicker if they live on one income (perhaps a higher one) and use the other income (perhaps a lower one) to pay off their mortgage. It is reported that this has enabled some couples to pay off their entire mortgage in a few years (Pant, 2021). Financial experts believe that living on one income in a two-income households gives them tremendous flexibility: more money to build savings, reduce debt, achieve other major goals, and have more options which can bring peace to their life (Lamberg, 2022).

### 5.8.2.  Avoiding trading up

As our need for space increases, it is tempting to buy a bigger house and take on a bigger mortgage. However, this will prevent us from achieving our goal of being mortgage free. The secret, as Warren Buffet, the billionaire, shows us, lies in keeping the cost of housing low by staying in the same house and not moving. Warren has lived in the same home for 65 years, which he bought in 1958 for $31,500 (DeVon, 2023). Although his house has five bedrooms, it is reported to be quite modest for a billionaire and is worth 0.003% of his total wealth (property is worth $1.4 million, and he has a net worth of over $120 billion) (Mancini, 2023).

With the surge in property prices and the costs of moving, it appears that more and more UK homeowners are following Warren's example and choose to improve their existing home rather than move to a new property when their needs change. Research carried out by Hiscox (specialist insurer) shows that the number of homeowners choosing to improve their homes rather than move has risen fivefold, from 3% in 2013 to 15% in 2018, representing more than four million households in the UK. Loft conversions, often seen as a cost-effective way to get more space, experience the highest level of growth, increasing by 114% between 2008 and 2017. Younger homeowners (18–34) are found to be most active home improvers, with 26% opting to renovate rather than move, compared with 8% of those over 55 (Hiscox, 2018, pp. 2–3).

### 5.8.3.  Regularly review your mortgage rates

As mortgage payments are often the largest household expense, it is important that you regularly review your rates. Most lenders allow you to secure a new rate three to six months before the end of your deal. It is therefore advisable to call your lender and explore your options with them before the end of your deal.

In looking at mortgage deals, you need to make two important decisions. The first decision is whether you want a product with or without an early repayment charge.

A product without an early repayment charge is useful in several scenarios:

- If you want to overpay your monthly mortgage payment by more than the normal limit permitted (lenders normally allow borrowers to overpay by 10% of the mortgage balance)
- If interest rate is likely to drop and you may wish to move to a cheaper deal
- If you may move, sell your property, and repay the whole loan

A mortgage product with no early repayment penalty offers flexibility, choice, and freedom and may be worth considering when the future is uncertain. A fixed product with no early repayment penalty is in many ways ideal because it gives an individual both certainty and flexibility.

By regularly reviewing your mortgage, you should be able to keep having competitive deals rather than remaining on a potentially more expensive standard variable rate.

### 5.8.4. Opting for lower fee

A second decision is whether an individual should opt for a lower interest rate product with a fee or a higher interest rate product with no fee. There are several factors that can help an individual make this decision:

- **How long does it take to recover the fee?**

You can use Table 5.3 to compare two deals and decide which one is cheaper.

- **Size of the loan**

The size of the loan affects the monthly savings. With a larger loan, a deal with a lower interest rate with a fee might work out cheaper than

Table 5.3 *Comparing mortgage deals with fee and no fee*

|  | *Lower interest rate with a fee* | *Higher interest rate with no fee* |
|---|---|---|
| Monthly mortgage payment |  |  |
| Fee divided by the length of the product (e.g. £999 on a 2 year deal is £999/24 months) |  | £0 |
| Total monthly cost |  |  |

a product with a higher interest rate with no fee. The earlier calculation will enable you establish which one is more cost-effective.

- **Investment returns**

Another consideration is the rate of return an individual could earn if they invested the fee. If the product fee is £999, and an individual invests this amount, how much return could they get? If an individual has a low-risk appetite and is unlikely to get a high return, then a low or no fee option is preferable.

- **Financial discipline**

The other consideration to take into account is financial discipline. Most lenders allow fees to be added to the loan, and so the mortgage amount borrowed increases and interest is payable on the fee. Unless there is an arrangement to pay this off (perhaps using the saving in the monthly mortgage cost as a result of choosing a cheaper deal), then the amount borrowed increases every time you change a deal.

If you go for a lower rate with a high fee, you will save on your monthly mortgage payment. However, whether this is a good option depends on your financial circumstances and how the monthly saving is used – is the money to be invested or spent? Without financial discipline, the monthly savings are likely to be spent. However, if you can make a good use of this surplus income (saving or overpaying the mortgage), then a high fee option is worth considering.

It is also advisable to contact an independent mortgage adviser to explore other options. Your lender can only offer you their products, but there might be a better and more suitable product with another lender. An independent mortgage adviser can explore options with other lenders and recommend a suitable deal.

### 5.8.5. Mortgage app

Technology can also help you manage your mortgage more effectively. Some apps, for example, are designed to assist homeowners in managing their mortgage more effectively by offering a simple and easy-to-understand platform where homeowners can track their mortgage payments and see the progress they're making.

They help users understand how even small additional payments can significantly impact their overall mortgage term and interest payments. For instance, some apps help homeowners visualise the cumulative impact of minor lifestyle changes, such as giving up a daily cup of coffee. By redirecting this small daily saving towards their mortgage, homeowners can see tangible results in the form of reduced interest and shortened loan terms.

Moreover, apps can also assist in finding the next best mortgage deal, simplifying the often complex process of mortgage shopping. It's designed to provide homeowners with the tools they need to make informed decisions, ultimately helping them achieve financial freedom sooner. However, apps may not give access to all lenders, and so you might not be able to use this technology yet. In the US, there are also a wide range of apps available to help homeowners manage their mortgage more effectively.

### 5.9. Conclusion

Mortgage payments are often our largest monthly expense. It is important to regularly review our loan to value and the mortgage deals on offer to ensure that we get the best possible deal. A first step in repaying our mortgage is taking control of it. This requires keeping our mortgage at the forefront of our mind, regularly reviewing the cost, and having a plan to pay it off.

Leveraging technology or apps can significantly streamline the management of your mortgage and assist you in finding the best deals. Numerous mortgage apps offer a range of features such as mortgage calculators, comparison tools, and reminders for payment deadlines. These digital tools can help you keep track of your payments, compare interest rates, and even identify opportunities for refinancing. By incorporating these tech solutions into your financial strategy, you can optimise your mortgage payments and potentially save a significant amount of money in the long run.

## References

Bank of England. (2020). Why more borrowers are choosing long-term fixed-rate mortgage products? Available at: www.bankofengland.co.uk/bank-overground/2020/why-are-more-borrowers-choosing-long-term-fixed-rate-mortgage-products [Accessed 12 July 2023].

Browning, S. (2023). Mortgage prisoners. *House of Commons Library Research Briefings.* Available at: https://researchbriefings.files.parliament.uk/documents/CBP-9411/CBP-9411.pdf [Accessed 12 July 2023].

Cribb, J., and Sturrock, D. (2022). Who is most affected by rising interest rates? *Institute of Fiscal Studies.* Available at: https://ifs.org.uk/articles/who-most-affected-rising-mortgage-interest-rates [Accessed 12 July 2023].

DeVon, C. (2023). Billionaire Warren Buffett still lives in the same home he bought for $31,500 more than 60 years ago. *CNBC.* Available at: www.cnbc.com/2023/03/03/warren-buffett-lives-in-the-same-home-he-bought-in-1958.html#:~:text=Billionaire%20Warren%20Buffett%20is%20famously,about%20%24329%2C505%20in%20today's%20dollars [Accessed 12 July 2023].

English Housing Survey. (2020). English Housing Survey: Headline report 2019–20. Available at: https://assets.publishing.service.gov.uk/government/uploads/system/uploads/attachment_data/file/945013/2019-20_EHS_Headline_Report.pdf [Accessed 12 July 2023].

English Housing Survey. (2021a). English Housing Survey: Headline report 2020–21. Available at: https://assets.publishing.service.gov.uk/government/uploads/system/uploads/attachment_data/file/1123670/2020-21_EHS_Headline_Report_revised_v2.pdf [Accessed 12 July 2023].

English Housing Survey. (2021b). English Housing Survey: Headline report 2021–22. Available at: www.gov.uk/government/statistics/english-housing-survey-2021-to-2022-headline-report/english-housing-survey-2021-to-2022-headline-report [Accessed 26 October 2023].

FCA. (2020). Mortgage switching research. Available at: www.fca.org.uk/publication/research/mortgage-switching-research.pdf [Accessed 12 July 2023].

Green, N. (2022). SVR mortgage confusion costs homeowners over £4k. *Unbiased.* Available at: www.unbiased.co.uk/news/mortgages/svr-mortgage-confusion-costs-homeowners-over-4k [Accessed 12 July 2023].

Hiscox. (2018). Hiscox renovations and extensions report 2018. Available at: www. hiscox.co.uk/sites/uk/files/documents/2018-03/Hiscox_renovations_ extensions_report_2018.pdf [Accessed 12 July 2023].

Jones, R. (2021). Offset mortgages: are they making a post-Covid comeback? Available at: www.theguardian.com/money/2021/jun/05/offset-mortgages-are-they-making-a-post-covid-comeback#:~:text=However%2C%20offset%20mortgages%20 appear%20to,you%20pay%20on%20your%20mortgage [Accessed 12 July 2023].

Lamberg, E. (2022). How (and why) to live on one income in a two-income household. Available at: www.realsimple.com/work-life/money/saving/live-on-one-income [Accessed 12 July 2023].

Mancini, J. (2023). Warren Buffett's $31,500 house is now worth $1.4 million but he says he would have made far more money by renting instead. Available at: https://finance.yahoo.com/news/warren-buffetts-31-500-house-181400983. html?guccounter=1&guce_referrer=aHR0cHM6Ly93d3cuZ29vZ2xlLmNvbS88&-guce_referrer_sig=AQAAADz5IoxfcgcgDz3hwDM6dHg_XDQHFeLquKvpmN-cU82-8zOVgA-d3Vrqwwmwe_uLNSxZ4A9daP5N9ZZMW7HlHO7wBGiG8H-3hBI50url-cERNe66a_9D5BGnohGYThMhHw5QOd9QujIEz9_p-y8gm-mrH-KYTmsY-5QgLxdDaEE2Ewf [Accessed 29 November 2023].

Otter, S. (2021). Couple in their 30s pay off £95k mortgage 28 years early with clever budgeting, *Manchester Evening News*. Available at: www.manchestereveningnews.co.uk/news/uk-news/couple-30s-pay-95k-mortgage-20779085 [Accessed 12 July 2023].

Pant, P. (2021). Why two-income couples should live with one paycheck. Available at: www.thebalancemoney.com/how-to-boost-savings-as-couple-453850 [Accessed 12 July 2023].

# Chapter Six
## Shield Your Wealth
### Mastering asset protection strategies

## 6.1. Introduction

A mortgage is often seen as a big burden because it involves keeping up with a financial commitment over a large part of our working life, commonly 25 years or more. Mortgages are built on the assumption that borrowers have stable employment and good health over a long period of time, allowing them to receive an undisrupted flow of income to meet mortgage payments. Yet, life is full of uncertainties, with everyone facing a daunting prospect of untimely death, poor health, and redundancy, resulting in a loss of income. Indeed, a loss of income is one of the main causes of mortgage difficulties, increasing the risk of repossession and homelessness.

The good news is that you can do something to ensure that life's uncertainties do not affect your ability to pay your mortgage and keep your home. There are three possible strategies for you to protect yourself: 1) build a financial buffer, 2) reduce the risk, and 3) transfer the risk to an insurance company. This chapter examines the risks you face and what you can do to mitigate them, so that you can avoid mortgage payment difficulties and the risk of losing your home.

DOI: 10.4324/9781003297765-6

## 6.2. Unlocking mortgage success: influential factors and risk-reduction techniques

It is difficult to establish the exact reasons why people fall into mortgage arrears, as these are likely to be complex, varied, and often result from a multiple of factors. Doling (1988) has broken down the factors into three categories. The first relates to structural factors such as income to loan ratios, interest rates, government subsidies, social security support levels, and loan to value ratios. The second concerns household income and expenditure factors, such as unemployment, short-term working, marital breakdown, sickness, unanticipated repairs, and other household expenditure. The third concerns personal factors such as money management skills, commitment to the house, and personal priorities (Doling, 1988). Some research finds that the most common reasons for mortgage difficulties are redundancy, a drop in earnings, small business failure, and relationship breakdown (quoted in Nettleton and Burrows, 1998, p. 736). The real cause relates to changes in income – from job loss, fluctuating income, or reduced incomes (Davies et al., 2016, p. 7). Research on arrears in Europe also shows that affordability problems (such as unemployment, low income, and high mortgage payments) are the main cause, but long-term arrears result from a combination of affordability problems and negative equity (Gerlach-Kristen and Lyons, 2017).

Changes in income are the key to explain mortgage arrears. This is supported by real-life stories from StepChange (debt advice). Carol was a freelance IT contractor/business analyst but was affected by the financial crisis of 2007. She had three months of emergency fund but did not have earnings for five months. Her sister helped her with a couple of mortgage payments and a friend with some bills, as she could not get help from the state as she was on an interest-only mortgage.

She built up debt, and her mental health declined, as she was being harassed by creditors who bombarded her with phone calls and sent debt collectors. Carol got in touch with StepChange who helped her devise a debt management plan so that she could be debt-free in four years (StepChange, 2023).

Sarah and Gary fell into financial difficulties as a result of a drop in earnings. Gary was a self-employed gardener and could not work for two months due to backache. As a result, they could not keep up with their mortgage payments and subsequently fell into mortgage arrears, which in turn affected their credit score. House prices were falling, which meant they could not borrow more from their home to cover their cash flow. Two days before Christmas, their house was repossessed, and they had to move into a rented property. Luckily, the rent was cheaper than their mortgage payment.

Embracing financial discipline, such as budgeting, setting up an emergency fund, saving 10–15% of income, and avoiding over-spending and debt, reduces the risk of falling into financial difficulties and ensures that you will always have a roof over your head. However, if you do face financial difficulties, it is advisable to contact a lender and charities for help.

In the following section, we will look at different risks facing homeowners and ways to mitigate them.

## 6.3. Life's uncertainties: balancing mortgages and the risk of premature death

It is important to protect ourselves and our family against the financial impact of death and illness risks because human capital is our biggest financial asset. Human capital can be defined as the present value of our future earnings and is determined by factors such as age, education, training, skills, and experience. Legal and General's Deadline to Breadline 2020 report found that 89% of people in the UK do not see themselves (their earning potential) as their biggest financial asset. They see their property, savings, and cars or vehicles to have a higher financial value, and this leads them to insure these assets, but not themselves.

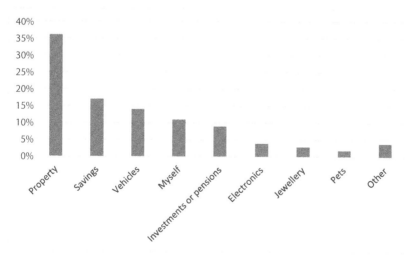

**Figure 6.1** *Perception of biggest assets in financial value*
*Source:* Adapted from L&G, 2020, p. 26

In reality, human capital is the biggest and most important asset any individual can own. In the UK, the average working household's annual income is just under £35,000, and so the average worker could earn over £1.4 million over 40 years (L&G, 2020, p. 26) These figures show that individuals are worth significantly more than the average home (average UK house price was £264,000 in April 2024), the average price of a used car (£16,964 in May 2024), and the average net household savings pot. The value of human capital, therefore, has been overlooked, and this explains the existence of a massive protection gap.

### 6.3.1. Premature death

Every household faces the risk of premature death, but the probability of death before the age of 65 in the UK is low (1% or less). However, every year many people die from road accidents and from lifestyle causes, such as smoking, alcohol, poor diet, lack of physical activity, and obesity.

Many people are worried about premature death because it can result in serious financial problems for the survivors due to the loss of the breadwinner's future earnings. This can give rise to economic insecurity and a reduction in standard of living if there is no adequate replacement income or financial assets to compensate. Premature death also results in additional expenses, such as funeral costs and non-economic loss such as grief and/or a loss of a role model.

The best tool to mitigate the risk of premature death is life insurance. Life insurance has been described as 'money to deal with death's financial fallout'. It is designed to provide survivors with financial resources to pay off debts and funeral expenses or replace the loss of income. It can play a powerful role in the transitionary life for survivors, by providing the necessary financial resources to enable them to avoid money worries, take time off work, and focus on grieving.

One of the key functions of life insurance is to provide a lump sum to settle any outstanding debts, such as a mortgage, to give survivors and dependents housing and financial security, and avoid homelessness and financial worries. In addition, life insurance can also provide the necessary fund to pay for funeral expenses to avoid debt and financial pressure on loved ones during an already-difficult time.

Life insurance also plays a crucial role in replacing lost income. A life insurance policy can pay out a lump sum or a monthly benefit to maintain the lifestyle of survivors and dependents.

Furthermore, it can be instrumental in covering death taxes (inheritance tax which has to be paid before the estate can be distributed), preventing these costs from diminishing the estate left to heirs.

Finally, for business owners or key individuals, life insurance can provide the necessary capital to help the business continue in their absence. Therefore, life insurance is a multifaceted tool, designed to offer financial protection and peace of mind across various aspects of life and beyond.

### 6.3.2. Death and the family home

The loss of a breadwinner can leave a family's housing security in jeopardy, especially if the mortgage hasn't been paid off or there is no life insurance in place to do so. A home carries emotional value, and most families wish to remain there after such a tragedy. Those with a fully paid mortgage enjoy stability knowing that they can continue living in their home, while others face uncertainty. Those with a life insurance policy have to wait before a claim is processed, and this may cause short-term cash flow issues. To expedite this, placing the policy in a trust ensures direct payment to beneficiaries or setting up in joint names in the case of couples.

As discussed in Chapter 3, families who have an outstanding mortgage but no life insurance face tough choices in times of grief: they may need to sell their home, move in with relatives, or resort to a quick sale at a reduced price (20–30% below market value). To secure peace of mind, it's vital to repay mortgages early or protect them with a life insurance policy held in a trust.

### 6.3.3. Funeral costs

The financial costs of dying also have a significant impact on families. In 2022, the average funeral cost in the UK was £9,200. However, SunLife's Cost of Dying Report 2023 shows that only 59% of the deceased put enough aside to cover the whole cost of their funeral, leaving the shortfall to be covered by family who are surprised by the high costs of certain items such as flowers, headstones, coffin, and catering. To cover these expenses, some dip into their savings and investments (33%), borrow money on credit cards (27%) or from friends and relatives (23%), sell possessions (15%), borrow from banks (14%), and pay funeral directors in instalments (12%) (Sun Life, 2023). *The Independent* newspaper reports that 43% of grieving adults have gone into debt or experienced financial hardship in

2022 after paying the cost of a funeral, as they have to contribute, on average, £1,800 of their own money and take on £1,900 of debt. This has a significant impact on their mental health, leaving family members feeling stressed (50%), anxious (45%), and embarrassed (36%) (Jenkins, 2022).

## 6.4. Types of life insurance

In the UK, there are three main types of life insurance – lump sum term assurance, whole of life, and family income benefit. In this section we will guide you through life insurance and family income benefit which are used as complementary solutions to provide money to meet capital and income needs.

### 6.4.1. Term assurance

A term assurance contract is designed to pay out a lump sum to enable a mortgage and debt to be paid off. It is a cost-effective solution because it is relatively cheap for two main reasons. First, the policy provides cover for a limited period: usually a term (e.g. 20 years, 30 years), or until an age (60 or 65), and therefore few claims are likely to be made as life expectancy in the UK is 80 or more. Second, term insurance provides pure insurance coverage as nothing is paid if the policy is cancelled or no claim is made during the policy term.

### 6.4.2. Whole of life policy

A whole of life policy is different from term assurance because it is designed to pay out on death whenever that happens. It is more expensive than term life insurance because it insures you for the whole of your life and is guaranteed to pay out. There are two types of policies: some have a premium guaranteed for life, and others have a premium which will be reviewed every five to ten years. A whole of life policy is often recommended to people who are likely to have an inheritance tax liability.

### 6.4.3. Term assurance – family income benefit (FIB)

While a term or a whole of life policy pays out a lump sum to enable survivors to pay off liabilities, they often have no income to live on and may be forced to live in relative poverty.

Years ago, the author met a widow who lost her husband in a car accident. On his death, his life insurance policy paid to her £200,000 which enabled her to pay off the mortgage. However, working part-time as a nurse on £20,000 per annum, her salary was insufficient to support four children. She had to sell the family home and moved to a smaller and cheaper house and used the difference to subsidise her living expenses. The life insurance industry uses the 'Widow Story' to underline the complimentary role of a family income benefit policy in family protection.

A family income benefit policy is designed to provide a replacement income to ensure survivors can maintain their standards of living when a breadwinner dies and a family loses its main source of income, to cover an ongoing expense (childcare/home help/nanny), or protect alimony payments in the event that the other party dies.

This policy is more affordable than a whole of life and a term life policy because it only provides an income, and the policy benefit is decreasing. For example, a family takes out a family income benefit policy to provide £20,000 of income for 20 years. If a claim is made in year one, a family receives payments for 20 years. If a claim is made in year 20, a family receives payments for one year. In other words, the number of years of payout is reduced with every year passes.

## 6.5. Defending your family's well-being and mortgage from health hazards

The risk of poor health – or more formally known as morbidity risk – is a far greater risk than the risk of premature death. In addition to the risk of injuries on the road, many people in the UK also suffer from work-related causes. The *Health and Safety Executive (HES)* reports that more than 1.8 million workers in the UK suffered from work-related ill health in 2021–2022 caused by stress, depression, or anxiety (51%), musculoskeletal disorders (27%), and other type of illness (22%), resulting in a loss of 36.8 million working days. The annual economic cost of work-related injury and new cases of ill health was estimated at £18.8 billion in 2019/2020. Mental health has also become a prominent issue – with 914,000 cases of work-related stress, depression, or anxiety in 2021/2022 (HSE, 2022).

The risk of developing a critical illness is also real. There are 7.6 million people living with heart and circulatory diseases in the UK (British Heart

Foundation, 2023), and 2.5 million with cancer, which is estimated to increase to 4 million by 2030 (Smith, 2020).

A critical illness causes financial strain on individuals, as they may not be able to work full-time, if at all, while their expenses rise. They might have to spend more money on healthcare costs, buy new clothes due to weight loss/gain, pay more for heating, and make adaptations to the home.

There are two types of policies to protect individuals against disability – income protection and critical illness. Income protection is designed to provide a replacement income during the whole of an individual's working life or a set period of years. Income protection insurance is costly, and so insurance companies now offer 'budget' policies as a cheaper alternative, which pay out for a shorter period (five years instead of a longer time).

### 6.5.1. Income protection policy

Many people are reliant on good health to be able to go to work and earn a living. If they fall ill and are unable to work, they would not receive an income. In order to maintain their standard of living and avoid poverty in the event of ill health, it is important to have a replacement income. Income protection policy, also called permanent health insurance, is designed to provide a replacement income when a policyholder is unable to work due to poor health. It covers being unable to work due to a wide range of conditions, from progressive illness (cancer), mental illness or depression, musculoskeletal problems, heart, blood pressure or blood circulation problems, stomach, liver, kidney or digestive problems, chest or breathing problems to stress. In 2022, nearly 16,000 people claimed against their individual income protection policies, representing a 9% increase from the previous year. Claims for musculoskeletal issues such as neck and back pain accounted for 34% (ABI, 2023). Other key reasons for the claim include cancer and increasing mental health.

An income protection policy can protect our income for the whole of our working life. Indeed, it can provide cover for more than 52 years, if the policy starts at age 18 and ends at age 70. Income protection insurance allows the insured to protect a large percentage of their income – commonly 50–70% – which is paid out tax-free. There is no limit on the number of claims you can make. However, many people do not have a policy in the UK, though some may receive this from their employer. In fact, it is reported that only around 6% of adults in the UK have an income protection policy, representing 3.6 million people (Ruzicka, 2022). The income protection gap is enormous. Swiss Re estimated that the income protection gap in the UK amounted to £175 billion of annual benefit in 2015. In 2017, this gap rose to an estimated £200 billion, and the total estimated 'protection gap' in the UK was £2.4 trillion (Contractor and Business Weekly, 2017).

The low uptake of income protection is partly due to a lack of awareness of the benefits. In a research on consumer perception of insurance carried out, respondents were asked to rank different types of insurance into categories of 'essential', 'sensible', and 'nice to have' (Roux, 2018). The results show that income protection is not seen as a priority, as can be seen in Figure 6.2.

Research by Aviva also indicates that 40% of parents in the UK do not think they ever need or want income protection (Aviva, 2017, p. 8).

In financial planning, protecting our income is essential as our livelihood is dependent on it. Income protection is the most important tool we have against long-term disability because it protects our income for the whole of our working life. If we cannot work due to ill health, an income protection policy provides a replacement income, allowing us to avoid a fall in

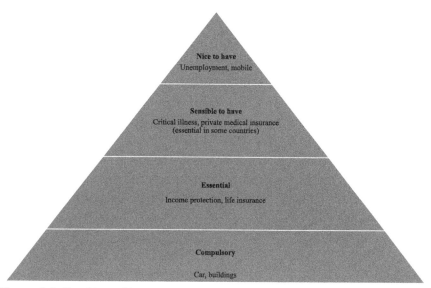

**Figure 6.2** *Rankings of insurance*
*Source:* Roux (2018)

living standards and poverty. Income protection has been aptly described as a wealth preservation tool, as in the event of long-term disability you will receive payments from an insurance company rather than deplete your savings. Figure 6.2 shows rankings of insurance.

However, an income protection policy may not offer a suitable solution for everyone. The policies are relatively expensive and have tight eligibility and claim criteria. The cost is determined by a wide range of factors, including age, occupation, smoker status, the length of term, benefit amount, deferred period (how long you have to wait from the onset of the condition to when the claim starts to be paid and often is dovetailed with sickness benefits employer provides), and medical history. In addition, the level of cover and premium are determined at the start of the policy, and so if earnings are lower at the point of claim, an individual may pay more for a policy.

### 6.5.2. Critical illness policy

Income protection pays a monthly income to enable you to meet expenses. However, you might also need a lump sum to pay off debts, or pay for treatments (e.g. speech therapy) and adjustments to the home (e.g. wheelchair access). A critical illness policy is designed to pay a one-off lump sum. A critical illness policy pays out on the diagnosis of a range of critical conditions (up to 40 or more conditions, and some insurers cover over 100), such as cancer, stroke, and heart attack. In 2019, according to the ABI, cancer was the biggest single reason for an individual critical illness claim. A critical illness policy often requires a 14- to 30-day survival period – that is, an individual must survive this period for the insurance company to pay out. If they do not survive the minimum period, there is no payout. For this reason, a critical illness policy is often combined with life insurance, so that payment will be made on a diagnosis of a critical condition or on death.

It is estimated that 9% of individuals in the UK have a critical illness policy, in comparison to 12% who have phone insurance. Royal London reported that 3.5 million people who were diagnosed with a critical illness between 2012–2017 were not able to cope financially (Royal London, 2017). Having a critical illness policy can help alleviate financial stress in times of need. Income protection and critical illness policies are complementary rather than alternatives, as one provides an income and the other a lump sum. Where budget is an issue, income protection is recommended because it covers more conditions (mental illnesses and back trouble) than critical illness and provides a regular income.

If financial resources were not an issue, it would be advisable to take out both a critical illness policy and an income protection policy. Where the ideal amount of cover is not affordable, it might be worthwhile to buy an amount which is within your budget.

## 6.6. Mortgage payment protection insurance

Besides income protection and critical illness cover, those with financial commitments may also wish to consider mortgage payment protection insurance (MPPI). This policy will pay a set amount each month, normally for a period of up to two years. There are three different types of policy: unemployment only, accident and sickness only, or accident, sickness, and unemployment (ASU). As an ASU policy is the most comprehensive, it is the most expensive. A mortgage payment protection insurance policy offers two types of cover. First, you can have a policy covering the cost of your mortgage payments only, or the cost of other bills too. In the case of the latter, the policy will typically cover 125% of your mortgage costs. Second, you can choose to base the cover on your salary and can protect up to 50% of your monthly salary. While a MPPI policy provides protection against three causes of income loss (unemployment, accident, and sickness), it is only a short-term policy, giving cover for up to 24 months. Income protection, on the other hand, is designed to provide protection against long-term illness.

## 6.7. Culture of low savings in UK

Protection is important because many families in the UK would struggle if they permanently lose a source of income, as they have inadequate safety nets and insufficient savings. Research by Legal and General shows that in the UK, households say that they need around £12,000 in savings to feel secure. However, many households do not have this level of savings: 60% of households have less than £5k in savings and 16% have no savings at all (this rises to one in three of those with an income of less than £20k). On average, Legal and General finds that a UK household has a net savings of £1,821, but 37% have less than £1,000 savings including 16% who have no savings at all. (Legal & General, 2022, pp. 6, 12). Another research shows that in 2022–2023, 48% of UK households had either no savings or less than £1,500 in savings. For single-parent households with children, this figure rises to 81% (Money Charity, May 2024, p. 16).

Based on their daily expenses, Legal and General calculates that on average, UK households have only 19 days' worth of savings (Legal & General, 2022, pp. 4, 8). In other words, many households are not able to support themselves for even one month if they lose their income.

Research shows that there is a positive relationship between savings and financial well-being, and therefore, by implication, low savings represent low financial well-being. There are two types of savings: short-term includes having an emergency fund, whereas long-term involves saving and investing for the future (e.g. retirement). Having money saved in an emergency fund enhances financial resilience by providing a buffer against financial shocks and the unexpected, while long-term savings increase financial security and confidence (Fan and Henager, 2022, pp. 417–418).

Financial planners typically suggest maintaining an emergency fund equivalent to at least three to six months' salary or income, depending on which is higher. However, some individuals may require a more substantial emergency fund, up to 12 months' worth, based on their circumstances and financial obligations. Factors to consider when determining the size of your emergency fund include job stability, number of dependents, debt obligations, and lifestyle expenses. Building up this fund ensures that you and your family can navigate challenging financial situations without compromising your overall financial well-being.

### 6.8. Inadequate and complex welfare benefits

Protection is also necessary because although there are welfare benefits available in the UK, the system is complicated and the benefits inadequate. Statutory sick pay (SSP), for example, is provided for up to 28 weeks for employees who are off work due to health or disability. Some employers provide sick pay on top of the statutory amount (known as additional occupational sick pay (OSP)). After SSP, employees may apply for employment and support allowance (ESA), if they have paid National Insurance for at least two years.

However, there are issues with the UK's sick pay system because

- SSP is limited to 28 weeks;
- the payment is equivalent to 17% of the average weekly household spending (Smith, 2020), creating a 83% shortfall; and
- after SSP ends, sick pay eligibility is means-tested and unclear.

The UK welfare system assumes that households will establish their own safety nets. However, the welfare system is complex and households need more guidance and information to enable them establish their safety net. Self-employed individuals face greater challenges as they aren't entitled to SSP, and ESA eligibility is means-tested and uncertain.

Employer and government sick pay provides some support, but to fully address your needs and circumstances, a private policy may be necessary to provide a longer recovery period and a higher income to maintain your lifestyle.

## 6.9. Protecting your property

In addition to protecting an individual's ability to earn an income, the property itself needs protection from damage, destruction and theft through fire, and flooding by taking out a policy called building insurance.

### 6.9.1. Building insurance

Building insurance typically provides coverage for a range of scenarios that may result in loss or damage to your property. These include fires, explosions, storms, floods, earthquakes, falling trees, theft, acts of vandalism, frozen or burst pipes. After September 11, terrorism insurance is offered by some insurers at an extra cost. When you buy building insurance, insurers can offer you insurance based on an unlimited sum to rebuild your property, or on actual the rebuild value of your property. The rebuild cost is stated in a valuation report prepared by a surveyor. It's essential to review your policy's terms and conditions to understand the extent of coverage, and any exclusions, and check your requirements with insurers.

### 6.9.2. Contents insurance

Home contents insurance provides protection against loss, theft, or damage to your personal belongings and household possessions. This cover typically includes items such as furniture, appliances, electronics, clothing, and other valuables within your home.

Additionally, home contents insurance can extend beyond the confines of your property, safeguarding certain possessions when you take them outside the home or on holiday. This feature, often referred to as 'personal possessions' or 'away from home' coverage, can protect items like jewellery, mobile phones, laptops, cameras, and other valuables that you might carry with you. As with any insurance policy, it's essential to review a policy's terms and conditions to understand what is covered and not covered (exclusions), and claim limits for specific items. Ensuring that your home contents insurance adequately covers your needs can provide peace of mind in the event of unexpected loss or damage to your belongings.

## 6.10. Conclusion

This chapter has examined some of the factors that contribute to difficulties in meeting mortgage payments and explored potential strategies to mitigate these challenges. By understanding these factors and implementing appropriate mitigation strategies, you can better manage your mortgage payments and maintain financial stability.

## References

ABI (2023). Protection insurers pay out £6.85 billion to support individuals and families. Available at: www.abi.org.uk/news/news-articles/2023/5/protection-insurers-pay-out-6.85-billion-to-support-individuals-and-families/ [Accessed 12 July 2023].

Aviva. (2017). Protecting our families. Available at: www.abi.org.uk/globalassets/files/appg/protecting-our-families-march-2017.pdf [Accessed 12 July 2023].

British Heart Foundation. (2023). Facts and figures. Available at: www.bhf.org.uk/what-we-do/news-from-the-bhf/contact-the-press-office/facts-and-figures#:~:text=There%20are%20around%207.6%20million,common%20type%20of%20heart%20disease [Accessed 12 July 2023].

Contractor and Business Weekly. (2017). The UK's £2.4 trillion protection gap. Available at: www.contractorweekly.com/insurance-news/uks-2-4-trillion-protection-gap/ [Accessed 12 July 2023].

Davies, S., Evans, J., Finney, A., and Hartfree, Y. (2016). Customer perspectives on mortgage arrears and advice seeking in Northern Ireland. Available at: https://bristol.ac.uk/media-library/sites/geography/pfrc/pfrc1709_customer-perspectives-on-mortgage-arrears.pdf [Accessed 8 June 2024].

Fan, L., and Henager, R. A. (2022). A structural determinants framework for financial well-being. *Journal of Family and Economic Issues*, 43, 415–428. Available at: https://link.springer.com/article/10.1007/s10834-021-09798-w [Accessed 12 July 2023].

Gerlach-Kristen, P., and Lyons, S. (2017). Determinants of mortgage arrears in Europe: Evidence from household microdata. *International Journal of Housing Policy*, 18 (4), 545–567. Available at: https://www.esri.ie/system/files/media/file-uploads/2017-10/JA201743.pdf [Accessed 8 June 2024].

HSE. (2022). HSE publishes annual work-related ill-health and injury statistics for 2021/22. Available at: https://press.hse.gov.uk/2022/11/23/hse-publishes-annual-work-related-ill-health-and-injury-statistics-for-2021–22 [Accessed 12 July 2023].

Jenkins, R. (2022). Two-fifths 'have gone into debt to pay for a funeral'. *Independent.* Available at: www.independent.co.uk/life-style/funeral-costs-uk-debt-b2232023. html [Accessed 12 July 2023].

Legal & General. (2022). Deadline to breadline 2022: Exploring the financial resilience of working households across the UK. Available at: https://www.legalandgeneral. com/landg-assets/adviser/files/protection/sales-aid/deadline-to-breadline-report-2022.pdf [Accessed 8 June 2024].

Money Charity. (2024). Money statistics May 2024. Available at: https://themoneycharity. org.uk/money-statistics/ [Accessed 8 June 2024].

Nettleton, S., and Burrows, R. (1998). Mortgage debt, insecure home ownership and health: An exploratory analysis. *Sociology of Health & Illness,* 20 (5), 731–753. Available at: https://onlinelibrary.wiley.com/doi/pdf/10.1111/1467-9566.00127 [Accessed 8 June 2024].

Roux, T. (2018). Understanding the protection gap in the UK Consumer research findings into protection insurance purchasing decisions. Available at: www.fs-cp. org.uk/sites/default/files/bdifferent_protection_research_final.pdf [Accessed 12 July 2023].

Royal London. (2017). Reality bites the cost of critical illness. Available at: https:// employer.royallondon.com/globalassets/docs/protection/brp8pd0004-critical-illness-report.pdf [Accessed 12 July 2023].

Ruzicka, A. (2022). Could you pay your bills if you couldn't work due to injury or illness? Only 6% of us have income protection insurance but it could prove vital. *Thisismoney.* Available at: www.thisismoney.co.uk/money/lifeinsurance/article-10579109/Can-pay-bills-work-disability-Heres-income-protection-important.html [Accessed 12 July 2023].

Smith, J. (2020). Critical illness cover. *Royal London.* Available at: https://studio.royal-london.com/docs/reportcic-example.pdf [Accessed 12 July 2023].

StepChange. (2023). Carol. Available at: www.stepchange.org/about-us/who-we-help/carol.aspx [Accessed 12 July 2023].

SunLife. (2023). Sunlife cost of dying report 2023. Available at: www.sunlife.co.uk/funeral-costs/#:~:text=69%25%20of%20people%20made%20provisions,%E2%80%93%20down%204%25%20since%202021 [Accessed 12 July 2023].

## Chapter Seven
## Utilising investments for mortgage repayment

### 7.1. Introduction

Mortgage-related investment issues are always topics of interest. Common questions clients often ask their financial advisers include: 1) should I pay down my mortgage faster? 2) should I invest inheritance or use it to pay off my mortgage? 3) should I take out equity from a property and invest in the stock market? (Tomlinson, 2002). This chapter discusses these questions and weighs up the trade-off between investing and paying off a mortgage.

### 7.2. Background

Investing to repay a mortgage, known as endowment mortgages, used to be the most popular mortgage repayment vehicle in the UK in the 1980s and 1990s. In 1988, 83% of new mortgages were endowment linked, with a total of more than 9 million endowment mortgages sold in the UK, and by mid-2000 some 23% of new mortgages were still endowment based (Edmonds, 2015, p. 4). With this type of mortgage, a house buyer would take out an interest-only mortgage with a lender and an endowment policy with an insurer. They paid a monthly premium to the insurer and expected a lump sum at the end of the term, usually 25 years, to repay the mortgage. The endowment policy also had a life

DOI: 10.4324/9781003297765-7

insurance element, so if the borrower were to die before the end of the term, a lump sum would be paid out.

The biggest attraction was that the endowment policy was expected to generate a lump sum greater than the required amount to pay off the mortgage, leaving borrowers with a surplus. However, changes in inflation rates over time meant that endowment mortgages became less suitable. With inflation at 15%–17% between the 1970s and early 1990s, endowment mortgages only needed to make a small return to generate nominal returns of 18%–20%. These returns would be used in promotional literature to persuade mortgage holders to take out an endowment mortgage. However, inflation fell (e.g. 4% in 2005), and the nominal returns of endowment policies declined proportionately. As a result, many policies sold ended up with a shortfall – one estimate suggested that 90% of the 9 million policies may have a shortfall of an average of £11,000, while the ABI calculated the average shortfall of £5,500 (Edmonds, 2015, pp. 4, 12, 13). This resulted in an endowment scandal, with more than 1.8 million endowment complaints lodged and compensation in excess of £2.7 billion made (Severn, 2008, p. 5).

As a product, an endowment policy was perceived as good, but the key issue was that consumers were not warned of the risk, and some consumers were poorly advised, as an assessment of the suitability of endowment policy was not made (Severn, 2008, pp. 5–6).

## 7.3. How to invest and repay mortgage early

Some academics argue that it may be more advantageous for some households to maintain a mortgage while also investing in a financial instrument. In their article discussing the comparison between 30-year and 15-year mortgages, Basciano et al. (2006) contend that for some borrowers, opting for a 30-year mortgage term combined with a concurrent investment plan could yield superior financial outcomes compared to choosing a 15-year mortgage term followed by an investment strategy. In other words, due to the power of compound interest, it is better to have an investment plan running simultaneously alongside a mortgage than to wait until the mortgage is paid off and then set up an investment plan. This works in two circumstances: 1) when mortgage rates are low and so investing is likely to generate a higher return; 2) when an individual has financial discipline and can put money aside. However, a major disadvantage with this approach is that it requires an individual to take risks, as they need to invest to produce a better financial outcome, and there are no guarantees that the strategy will produce higher returns.

### 7.3.1. Invest monthly savings

There are two possible ways for homeowners to invest to repay their mortgage early: invest monthly savings or lump sum. Before the financial crisis of 2008, interest-only mortgages were popular, but many of these deals were withdrawn as a result of the crisis.

With an interest-only mortgage, borrowers pay a lower monthly payment and could invest the monthly payment difference in an investment vehicle to enable them to accumulate a lump sum to repay their mortgage. This could enable them to repay their loan sooner than with a traditional mortgage. For example, a borrower with a £100,000 traditional mortgage over 25 years at 5% mortgage rate would pay £585 a month in repayments but only £417 on an interest-only deal, giving a monthly saving of £168. If the homeowner invested the £168 per month and achieved a return of 7% per year, their investment would grow to £136,885 after 25 years. This would allow them to pay off their mortgage and have £36,885 left over. Alternatively, they could pay off their mortgage roughly four years earlier once their investments reach £100,000.

However, this strategy involves several risks. First, there is an investment risk. If investment returns were lower than their mortgage rate, there would be a shortfall. For example, if investment growth rate is 4.5%, they would receive a return of £93,252 after 25 years, leaving a shortfall of £6,748. The shortfall might be larger if investment fee is included. If the gross investment return is 4.5% and fee is 0.5%, the net investment return is 4%. At 4% net investment growth rate, the sum accumulated at the end of 25 years amounts to £86,661, giving a shortfall of £13,339.

Second, a rise in interest rate would lower the amount available to invest as they have to spend more on interest and servicing the debt. Third, the borrower is exposed to market risk. If the stock market crashes, this could leave borrowers with a significant shortfall. There is also the risk of negative equity as a borrower is not reducing the debt, and if house prices fall, they could end up owning more than the home is worth. Taking into account these risks, a less risky approach is to use the overpayment facility.

### 7.3.2. Invest lump sum

A borrower may also have a lump sum which they wish to use to pay off their mortgage. However, the question of whether to pay off their mortgage early or invest needs to be viewed in a wider context of the financial situation of the borrower. Sam, 35, for example, wants to pay off his mortgage as early as possible. He has approximately £275,000 in outstanding mortgage debt, with a monthly repayment of £1,280, and expects to pay off his mortgage by the age of 55. He also has £40,000 in spare cash. However, he is changing his job, and the new salary is around 50% less.

In this situation, the borrower might wish to consider the following:

a) **The overall financial situation**: overpaying a mortgage means turning cash into brick and mortar and taking money out of a property again is more challenging with a job change and a drop in salary. An individual going through a career change may wish to wait until future income is clear and keep mortgage agreements as flexible as possible.

b) **Protection:** changing job also requires a review of protection needs, as a new employer might not offer the same benefits. In addition, a reduction in salary means death in service benefit is lower and so life insurance need may require a review.

c) **Emergency fund**: setting up an emergency fund is recommended to provide financial security. Although financial advisers typically recommend putting aside 3–12 months of expenditure or income, the amount should be tailored to an individual's personal circumstances.

d) **Investing**: it is possible to invest some of the cash to grow this to a suitable lump sum to repay a mortgage.

e) **10% overpayment:** it is possible to overpay a mortgage by 10%.

f) **Review mortgage options**: an individual may wish to review mortgage options.

In short, before using a lump sum to pay off a mortgage, we need to consider our overall financial situation and other financial goals.

Bill has a repayment mortgage of £140,000 and has £47,000 of savings. He has a £10,000 loan for home renovations, and £4,000 credit card debt. He has recently left his job to become freelance. Bill wonders whether he should pay down his mortgage or invest any spare cash?

In this situation, Bill may wish to consider:

a) **Emergency fund:** with no regular income, it is even more important to have an emergency fund.
b) **Protection needs:** leaving a job means losing a few potential employee benefits, including death in service, pension, holiday pay, and sick pay. Protection needs (income protection, critical illness, and life insurance) should be reviewed because long-term goals are often reliant on continued ability to work.
c) **Pay off expensive debts:** mortgage is the cheapest form of borrowing, and other debts (loan and credit card) should be repaid first.
d) **Offset mortgage:** an offset mortgage provides access to the cash while saving interest on mortgage.

Ann, 58, also wonders whether to use £136,000 inheritance to pay off her mortgage of £53,000 with nine years left. She is on a fixed rate deal and would have to pay a penalty if she pays off her mortgage. Before a decision can be made, Ann needs to contact her lender to find out when her current deal ends and how much she has to pay the lender if she wishes to clear the mortgage now. If the early repayment penalty charge is high, she may need to wait until the fixed rate deal ends. In the meantime, she could put the money in an ISA, or savings account, to earn interest.

Some financial advisers recommend adopting a less binary approach and invest money across different pots rather than taking an either or attitude. David, aged 55, is a higher-rate taxpayer and inherits £450,000. He has a fixed rate mortgage at 3% with an outstanding balance of £330,000, and there is £15,000 early redemption penalty. He therefore could consider the following:

a) **10% overpayment facility:** it is possible to reduce outstanding mortgage using the 10% facility to avoid paying the early redemption penalty.
b) **Invest in stocks and shares ISAs:** if interest rate is relatively low, investing the money might be beneficial if an individual has a risk appetite.
c) **Pension contributions:** as a higher-rate taxpayer, contributing to a pension could be beneficial as individuals receive 40% tax relief.

In short, before paying off a mortgage, homeowners should have the following in place:

a)  **Protection**: a homeowner should have suitable protection in place to ensure a mortgage can be repaid in the event of premature death and a mortgage payment can be met in the event of sickness and illness.

b)  **Emergency fund:** establish an emergency fund equivalent to six months' expenditure or more, depending on their circumstances, and keep the money in cash or an easy access savings account.

c)  **Pay off expensive debts**: unsecured debts tend to be expensive, and so it is recommended to pay off these debts first, including overdrafts, credit cards, and loans. With regards to mortgage debt, there is a stronger argument for paying it off when mortgage rates are increasing but check penalties before making this decision.

## 7.4. General considerations

In considering the trade-off between investing and paying off the mortgage, there are a few factors to take into account. The first is the desire for simplicity. Paying off the mortgage is simple and avoids complexity. Even though it might be possible to generate a higher return than the mortgage rate, some homeowners may not want the trouble, preferring a simple life without the emotional stress of worrying about the rise and fall of their investments.

The second is attitude to risk. Investing involves taking a host of risks including investment (the value might fall) and shortfall (the amount generated inadequate) risks. Risk-adverse individuals are therefore advised to pay off their mortgage. There is also the capacity for risk to consider. Even though an individual may be willing to take the investment risk, their financial situation might prevent them from taking such a risk, because of the detrimental impact on their lifestyle should the investment not work out. This is known as capacity for risk. For example, a couple – a manual worker and his wife – purchased an endowment mortgage in the 1980s to buy their council house. They saved £6,000 during their working lives from their small income, but their endowment mortgage had a shortfall of £3,000. They, therefore, had to use half of their life savings – money that they had put aside for their retirement over 30 to 40 years – to pay off their mortgage (Lucas, 2002). This example shows that the couple had a low capacity for risk, as the poor outcome affected their lifestyle in retirement, and would have been better off with a repayment mortgage.

Another example can be used to demonstrate this point. A businessman has a house with no mortgage worth £1.5 million and also £3 million worth of investments. He has sold a successful business worth a few millions. He would like to invest £500,000. As he could get a mortgage at 1%, he was advised to borrow against his home rather than cash in his investments, which are expected to generate higher returns. This example shows that the individual can take risks as he has a high capacity for risk and can deal with the negative consequences if things do not work out as planned.

A third issue is the time horizon. Investments can be volatile in the short term, and so investing for a short length of time (less than ten years) to accumulate a lump sum to repay a mortgage amount is not advisable. This means that investing may be more suitable for younger homeowners and generally not for those approaching retirement.

The fourth issue is the long-term investment outlook and whether the stock market is expected to perform well in the future or not. For example, if the market outlook is that the economy is likely to enter a recession and interest rates will rise, paying off the mortgage is a safer option. However, if returns are expected to be high while mortgage interest rates remain stable, taking an investment risk might bring rewards.

Fifth, investing a large sum may require financial advice, and this involves paying a fee and spending time to formulate an investment strategy. Investing is complex as there is so much choice. Consumers may need the assistance of a financial adviser to help them choose suitable investments. A financial adviser needs to assess their financial situation and attitude to and capacity for risk before making a suitable recommendation. The process can also be time-consuming and expensive.

## 7.5. Specific factors

In addition to the general considerations earlier, there are three other factors that can affect the decision. The first concerns mortgage interest rates – the lower the rate, the greater the differential between the cost of the mortgage and the potential return we can achieve from investing, while the higher the mortgage rate, the lower the differential.

In China, a fall in mortgage rate has encouraged homeowners on a more expensive deal to repay their mortgage early by tapping into their personal savings or taking out a cheaper loan. It is estimated that nearly $700 billion of mortgages (1/8 of China's outstanding total) have been repaid between 2022–2023. A bank in Beijing reports that 20% of existing clients has applied to repay their mortgage. This has affected banks' profits on mortgages (Tang et al., 2023). One homeowner plans to pay off her 25-year mortgage in five years, which will save her close to 1 million yuan (US$140,535) in interest payments. She pays 5.1% interest on her mortgage and, with the slump in equity markets, does not believe that there are investment products that can give her a higher return (Liu, 2022). She therefore decides to use her savings and surplus income to pay off her mortgage.

Second, the income tax rate of homeowners also affects the decision. In the UK, mortgage payments no longer receive interest relief, unlike other countries like the US and Australia. This means that we pay our mortgage after we pay tax, and therefore the gross mortgage rate is higher than the advertised headline rate. As Table 7.1 shows, a mortgage rate of 5% represents an investment return equivalent to 6.25% for 20% taxpayer, 8.3% for 40%, and 9% for 45%. Investment returns need to be higher than these rates to be attractive – for example, 9% net return to be attractive for a 45% taxpayer.

The third factor is the level of investment return, which is influenced not only by the attitude to risk but also approach to investment, as well as costs associated with the investments and taxation. The costs of investing include financial advice fee, commission, annual management fee, fund charge, platform fee, and performance fee. Investments are also subject to income tax (rate varies according to income tax position), capital gains tax, and inheritance tax. In other words, investing is much more complex than overpaying or paying off a mortgage, and needs knowledge, research, and time to ensure a positive return.

**Table 7.1** *Mortgage interest rates and income tax rates*

| Mortgage interest rate | Gross mortgage rate if income tax rate 20% | Gross mortgage rate if income tax rate is 40% | Gross mortgage rate if income tax rate is 45% |
|---|---|---|---|
| 3.50% | 4.40% | 5.80% | 7.80% |
| 5% | 6.25% | 8.30% | 9.00% |

*Source:* Author's calculations

## 7.6. Why fees matter in investing

It is important to consider investment fees and their impact on the over-all return. An investor might see a 2% fee and dismiss it as insignificant. However, a fee expressed as a percentage does not reveal the true cost.

Table 7.2 shows that a £100,000 investment over 25 years at 7% with 0.5% can generate a sum of £482,000. However, this falls to £429,000, representing a loss of 11% if annual fee rises to 1%, 30% loss if fee rises to 2%, and 38% loss if fee is 2.5%. There is a perception that higher-cost funds are likely to produce a superior annual return. However, research shows that on average, lower-cost funds tend to produce better future results than higher-cost funds, and that the cheapest equity funds out-perform the most expensive ones across five-, ten-, 15-, and 20-year periods.

## 7.7. Approaches to investing

There are two approaches to investing – active and passive. Active invest-ing is an investment strategy that involves frequent trading of individual shares with the aim of beating average index returns. This means that active managed funds tend to be more expensive, due to higher invest-ment expenses, transaction costs, and taxes (e.g. tax or duty). However, research shows that most fund managers fail to beat market benchmarks.

Dimensional Fund Advisors (DFA) seeks to offer better returns by draw-ing upon the works of Professors Eugene Fama (University of Chicago) and Kenneth French (Dartmouth), two Nobel laureates and financial econo-mists. This shows that it is possible to obtain more attractive returns by investing in equity, and over-weighting the exposure of a portfolio to value

**Table 7.2** *Investment fees and their impact on overall returns*

| Amount of investment | Time horizon | Investment return | Annual fee | Net return after annual fee | Total return |
|---|---|---|---|---|---|
| £100,000 | 25 years | 7% | 0.50% | 6.50% | £482,000 |
| £100,000 | 25 years | 7% | 1% | 6% | £429,000 |
| £100,000 | 25 years | 7% | 2% | 5% | £338,000 |
| £100,000 | 25 years | 7% | 2.5 | 4.50% | £300,000 |

*Source:* Author's calculations. Note: only use round numbers.

stocks (underpriced), small cap stocks (shares of small companies tend to outperform large-cap but more volatile and riskier), and stocks with recent strong price momentum (high trading volumes) and strong profitability growth. However, these funds are only available through financial advisers, and so advisory fees will need to be paid on top of the fund fees.

Passive investing, on the other hand, is a strategy that focuses on purchasing shares of index funds or ETFs that aim to duplicate the performance of major market indices and buying and holding assets for the long term. Passive investing does not require daily attention, so transactions and fees are lower. Some financial advisers have a strong bias towards index funds and prefer to stay away from actively managed funds because the latter requires making two bets: 1) that the market will do well and 2) that the fund manager will be able to outperform the market, and the amount will be more than enough to offset the extra costs and taxes.

## 7.8. Individual savings accounts (ISAs)

Tax efficiency is also important in determining net returns. Investments are subject to three taxes – income tax, capital gains tax, and inheritance tax. While inheritance tax is the same for all groups of taxpayers, income tax on dividends ranges between 8.75% to 39.35% and capital gains tax 10% to 20%.

One way to invest tax efficiently is investing in an individual savings account (ISA). Every year, adults over 18 are allowed to contribute £20,000 into an ISA. ISA funds are accessible and can be used at any time to pay off a mortgage because there are no time restrictions, unlike pensions where accessibility is available only after a certain age. Long-term investing has the potential to significantly increase an individual's wealth. In the UK, there were more than 4,000 ISA millionaires in 2021 (Ross, 2023). Hargreaves Lansdown, one of the top investment

Table 7.3 *Types of taxes*

| Types of tax payers | Income tax on dividends | Capital gains tax on investments | Inheritance tax |
|---|---|---|---|
| Basic rate – 20% | 8.75% | 10% | 40% |
| Higher rate – 40% | 33.75% | 20% | 40% |
| Additional rate – 45% | 39.35% | 20% | 40% |

*Note:* individuals are entitled to a CGT allowance before paying CGT

platforms in the UK, has 626 ISA millionaires with an average age of 74. With the youngest at 39, this suggests that it is possible to become an ISA millionaire in 21 years by investing the maximum allowance of £20,000 each year and achieving at least 7% investment growth per year. The platform also shares three secrets of success of their ISA millionaires including investing as much as possible early in the tax year, holding collective investments rather than single shares, and diversifying geographically (Coles, 2023). The keys to investment success lie in investing early, maximizing investments, and diversifying.

## 7.9. Conclusion

Deciding whether to pay off a mortgage or invest depends on an individual's financial situation. Before making risk-associated decisions, borrowers should establish an emergency fund, settle high-interest debts, and secure appropriate insurance. Once these measures are in place, a diverse financial strategy can be considered, including overpaying a mortgage, investing in an ISA, and contributing to a pension plan, to achieve financial security and growth.

## References

Basciano, P. M., Grayson, J., and Walton, J. (2006). Is a 30-year mortgage preferable to a 15-year mortgage? Available at: www.researchgate.net/publication/26437005_Is_a_30-Year_Mortgage_Preferable_to_a_15-Year_Mortgage [Accessed 12 July 2023].

Coles, S. (2023). Investing like a millionaire – our ISA millionaires' most popular funds. *Hargreaves Lansdown*. Available at: www.hl.co.uk/news/articles/investing-like-a-millionaire-our-isa-millionaires-most-popular-funds [Accessed 27 October 2023].

Edmonds, T. (2015). Endowment mortgages, House of Commons Library, Briefing Paper, Number 570. Available at: https://researchbriefings.files.parliament.uk/documents/SN00570/SN00570.pdf [Accessed 12 July 2023].

Liu, P. (2022). Chinese homeowners in a rush to clear mortgages early as consumers turn pessimistic over economic outlook. *South China Morning Post*, 10 October. Available at: www.scmp.com/business/china-business/article/3195151/chinese-homeowners-rush-clear-mortgages-early-consumers [Accessed 12 July 2023].

Lucas, I. (2002). Endowment mortgages. Available at: www.theyworkforyou.com/whall/?id=2002-07-16.45.0 [Accessed 12 July 2023].

Ross, M. (2023). Number of Isa millionaires nearly triples in one year. Available at: www.telegraph.co.uk/money/investing/isas/number-isa-millionaires-nearly-triples-one-year/#:~:text=The%20number%20of%20Isa%20millionaires,the%202019%2D20%20tax%20year [Accessed 27 October 2023].

Severn, D. (2008). The Financial Ombudsman Service and mortgage endowment complaints. Available at: www.financial-ombudsman.org.uk/files/17744/DavidSevern-Report.pdf [Accessed 12 July 2023].

Tang, Z., Gao, L., and Woo, R. (2023). Analysis: China's mortgage rate cuts spur prepayment rush, threaten bank earnings. *Reuters*, 20 February. Available at: www.reuters.com/markets/asia/chinas-mortgage-rate-cuts-spur-prepayment-rush-threaten-bank-earnings-2023–02–17/#:~:text=Analysts%20estimate%20that%20nearly%20%24700,started%20to%20lower%20borrowing%20rates [Accessed 12 July 2023].

Tomlinson, J. A. (2002). Advising investment clients about mortgage debt. *Journal of Financial Planning*, 15 (6), 100–108.

CHAPTER EIGHT

DECIDING BETWEEN PAYING OFF MORTGAGE AND
BOOSTING PENSION SAVINGS

## 8.1. Introduction

Some experts argue that a better option for some borrowers is to make contributions into a pension plan rather than paying off their mortgage. In a study on the trade-off between mortgage payments and retirement savings, the authors show that 38% of US households who accelerate their mortgage payments instead of saving for retirement make a wrong choice and lose as much as $1.5 billion per year. The authors calculate that reallocating their savings can result in an average benefit of 11 to 17 cents per dollar (or 11–17% return), depending on the choice of investments (Amromin et al., 2007).

Calling this behaviour 'inefficient', they blame debt aversion and risk aversion for the making the wrong choice, preferring to pay off debt obligations early rather than take advantage of tax-advantaged investments. For example, debt-averse households may find it more appealing to make a mortgage repayment, directly reducing their debt, even though it might lead to a lower net worth than to make a pension contribution. More risk-averse households also may choose to forgo an increase in expected wealth because making a pension contribution requires taking risks. In addition, they may be motivated by a 'socially acceptable' savings goal like debt-free homeownership (Amromin et al., 2007). This eliminates their desire to consider other alternative investment choices.

DOI: 10.4324/9781003297765-8

This chapter looks at the trade-off between making additional mortgage payments and contributing into a pension plan. It starts first with an examination of the importance of retirement planning.

## 8.2. Importance of retirement planning

Saving for retirement has become increasingly critical for several reasons. First, a rise in life expectancy means that many of us will spend an extensive number of years in retirement (possibly 30 years or more), and so more money will be required to fund a longer life. The amount needed is substantial and means that contributions need to start early to be affordable by taking advantage of compound interest. Second, changes in state and occupational pension provision means that the responsibility for saving and investing for retirement has increasingly shifted to individuals. Third, evidence indicates that some people are unable or unwilling to continue working beyond the age of 50–55, and therefore saving for retirement needs to occur in earlier years.

Changes in the State Pension in the UK mean that individuals need to take greater responsibility for their own retirement. One of the most important reforms is the increase in the State Pension age (SPA), or the age when individuals become entitled to a State Pension. Between 1940 and 2010, the SPA was 65 for men and 60 for women in the UK, but by 2020 this was equalised to 66 for both men and women. The government is considering a further rise in the future. Individuals need to have a minimum of ten qualifying years to receive some State Pension and 35 qualifying years for the full amount.

Demographic and social changes and the resulting financial pressures have made these changes necessary worldwide. In the UK, for example, the State Pension was first introduced in 1908 when life expectancy at birth was 40 years for men and 43 years for women, and only 24% of people reached the State Pension age of 70. For those reaching 70, they lived, on average, another nine years. However, State Pension was means-tested, not a universal benefit, and so not everyone received a State Pension even if they lived to the State Pension age. By 2016–2017, demographic changes have made the State Pension unsustainable: life expectancy at birth had more than doubled, to 84.1 years for men and 86.9 years for women, and around 85% of people reached their state pension age. The State Pension is a universal benefit and not means-tested, and so the government supports the retirees, on average, for

24 years (PPI, 2017). This exerts a tremendous pressure on government spending, with pensioner benefit spending reaching 11.5% of total public spending or 5.3% of GDP by 2023–2024 (OBR, 2023). In response to these financial pressures, the government is considering raising the State Pension age to 68 by 2039 (DWP, 2023). This age is relatively low in comparison to other OECD countries who plan to raise the state pension age beyond 70. Denmark plans to raise their retirement age from 65.5 to 74 years, Estonia from 63.8 to 71 years, and Italy from 62 to 71 years (OECD, 2023). Other OECD countries have extended or plan to extend the working life.

The rise in state pension age is a great concern for individuals for two key reasons: first, state pension is a primary and only source of income for a significant proportion of people (39% in UK (Dunstan, 2022)), and without this, they would not have a means to support themselves in retirement. Second, some individuals may not be able to work until their state pension age due to health reasons, and this group may need to save even more during the period when they are able to work.

In the UK, around 27% or more than 3.5 million people aged between 50 and 64 are currently economically inactive due to personal choice, redundancy, desire for lifestyle change, stress, caring responsibilities, job dissatisfaction, illness, loss of job, mental health, and disability (ONS, 2022). Of the 3.5 million, around 1.4 million people (40%) are inactive because of long-term sickness. Those who have poor health have lower wealth (total of pension, property, financial, and physical assets) than other groups – £57,000 in comparison to £137,000 for those who stop work to look after family, and £1.24 million for those who choose to retire early (Phoenix, 2023). Research by ONS also confirms that those who choose to retire early tend to be reasonably well-off – two-thirds (66%) owned their homes without any outstanding mortgage in August 2022 (ONS, 2022a). In other words, for some people, the saving period is much shorter, 29–34 years (from the age of 16–21 to 50) rather than 50 years (from age 16–66) and means that the amount of saving needs to be higher to achieve the same target. In addition, their desired retirement lifestyle might be more expensive, requiring more money to be saved.

Changes in occupational pensions have also shifted the responsibility of saving and investing for retirement to individuals. Previously, many individuals were members of a defined benefit pension scheme, where employers bear all the risks and offer a guaranteed income in retirement.

Increasing life expectancy, poor investment performance, ongoing funding commitment, and regulatory pressures led employers to shift the responsibility for providing retirement income to employees by enrolling them into a defined contribution pension scheme.

Under a defined contribution pension, individuals accumulate a pension pot which they can use to buy an income (e.g. annuity), or they can withdraw an amount when they reach retirement. This means that a defined contribution pension introduces a host of risks, including investment (value of pension fund might fall), annuity (rates might change), and longevity risk (running out of money). In 2008, for example, Tina had a defined contribution pension plan and planned to retire. However, the stock market was falling as a result of the global financial crisis, and so her pension fund lost 30%, forcing her to work five years longer.

Individuals might not be able to achieve their goal because they do not take enough risks with their investment. The World Economic Forum reports that Japanese only have savings to support 4.5 years in retirement, because they do not take enough risks and therefore receive a lower return than otherwise (WEF, 2019, p. 21). Changes in state and occupational pensions mean that the quality of life in the years before and during retirement will now depend critically on an individual's ability to save, invest, and take investment risks.

## 8.3. How much income is required in retirement?

The shift from defined benefit to defined contribution pension also raises a difficult question of how much individuals need to save for their retirement. One universal method to determine consumption/income need in retirement is the use of replacement rates, which specify the percentage of pre-retirement income that would enable individuals to maintain a similar lifestyle. The Geneva Association, for example, uses a replacement rate of 60% while WEF 70%, which is in line with the OECD guidelines. Replacement rates, however, can be higher, at 75%, 80%, 90%, or even 100%. WEF argues that low-income workers, for example, will need an income replacement rate closer to 100%, while higher-income workers will require less (WEF, 2017, p. 8). In general, individuals are assumed to require a lower income in retirement because certain expenses (e.g. mortgage payments, costs of raising children) are no longer payable.

It is easier for individuals to calculate their income in retirement under a defined benefit pension because this is based on a formula. For example, a 1/60 scheme means that an individual needs to work 30 years to receive 50% of their pre-retirement income, and a 1/80 scheme 40 years. Under a defined contribution pension, individuals build up a pension pot, and it is more difficult to know how much they need. A number of organisations offer targets guidelines using the principle of a multiple of salary. Fidelity Investments suggests saving ten times a person's annual salary by the age of 67 (Fidelity Investments, 2023). For example, someone earning £30,000 per year should have £300,000 by the age of 67. Aon (a global consulting company) recommends a slightly higher target of 11.1 times final pay by age 67 (Bond and Doonan, 2020, p. 2; Retirement Income Journal, 2022). While this approach is easy to understand, it is difficult to establish whether this amount is sufficient to support a desired lifestyle and expenditure.

The Retirement Living Standards, set up in 2019 by the Pension and Lifetime Savings Association, seeks to help individuals understand the lifestyle they want in retirement and the costs of these. It establishes three levels of expenditure: minimum, moderate, and comfortable (while the consumer organisation *Which* uses basic, comfortable, and luxury) and gives a breakdown for each, which could help an individual fine-tune their income target, as shown in Figure 8.1.

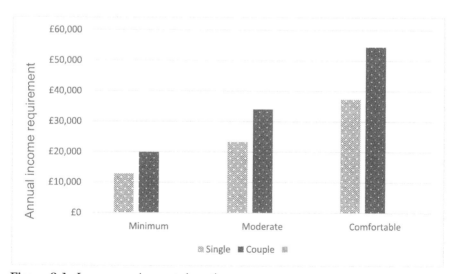

**Figure 8.1** *Income requirements in retirement*
*Source:* Adapted from Retirement Living Standards, 2023

a) **A minimum income target** requires £12,800 for someone who is single and £19,900 for a couple and covers spending on food and drink (excluding meals out), housing payments (mortgage payments, rent, or council tax), transport, utility bills, insurance, household goods, phone broadband, clothes, shoes, and health products. However, there is no budget for a car.

b) **A moderate income target** requires £23,300 for someone who is single and £34,000 for a couple, and includes the essentials mentioned earlier, plus regular short-haul holidays, recreation and leisure, tobacco, gifts to family and friends, alcohol, and charity donations, as well as the costs of running a second-hand car (replaced every ten years).

c) **A comfortable income target** requires £37,300 for someone who is single and £54,500 for a couple, which covers all the spending mentioned earlier, plus extended or long-haul holidays, health club memberships, home improvements, private healthcare, a new car every five years, and the costs of having a second, used car (replaced every five years).

As the minimum income target has no budget for a car, individuals who depend on this may need to aim for a higher income target (moderate or comfortable). While these guidelines help individuals understand the cost of each lifestyle, they still need to establish whether they have a shortfall and how much extra they need to save.

## 8.4. Why private savings are necessary?

Saving for retirement is necessary because state pensions are insufficient to meet income needs. As Figure 8.2 shows, the UK State Pension only covers the needs of a couple living outside London, as they receive £21,200 of state pension (assuming full entitlement for the new State Pension) while their income target is £19,900. All other groups face a shortfall between what they need and what they receive from the government. The shortfall ranges between £2,200 per year for a single individual targeting the minimum income lifestyle, to £35,300 for a couple living in London wanting a comfortable lifestyle.

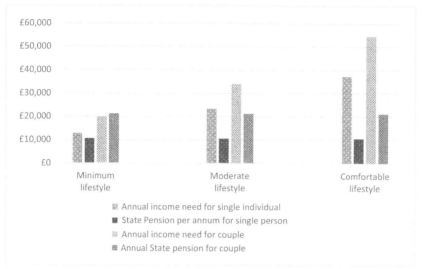

**Figure 8.2** *State pension inadequate to pay for costs of living*
*Source:* Data from Retirement Living Standards, 2023

## 8.5. How much do individuals need to save per month?

Research suggests that homeowners may need to save less than renters to maintain their living standards in retirement. It is suggested that homeowners need a pension pot of £260,000 (equivalent to £13,000 of income per year based on a 5% annuity rate), while private renters £445,000 (equivalent to £22,000 of income per year based on a 5% annuity rate) (ONS, 2020). We can use these figures to give an indicative amount of how much an individual would need to save per month.

Figure 8.3 shows that the earlier an individual saves for retirement, the lower the monthly contribution required due to the power of compound interest. If a homeowner begins saving at the age of 20, the monthly contribution is £64 in comparison to £111 for renters. If they wait until the age of 60, the monthly contribution jumps more than 16 times to £1,068 (or £1,830 for renters). This means that individuals should not wait until they have finished repaying their mortgage before beginning to save for retirement. They need to save and invest as early as possible to make the monthly contribution affordable, and a pension plan should be running concurrently alongside a mortgage.

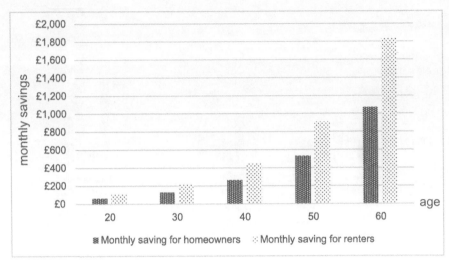

**Figure 8.3** *Importance of saving early – age and monthly pension contribution (Assumption: 7% investment return and retirement at 65)*
*Source:* Author's calculations

## 8.6. Benefits of saving in a pension fund

One significant benefit of saving in a pension fund is tax relief on contributions, designed to encourage individuals to save for retirement. This reduces the tax you pay, gives an instant boost to your savings, and helps the fund grow faster than other kinds of investment. The maximum contribution is equivalent to 100% of earned income or up to a specified amount. If you have no earnings, you can still contribute to a pension plan, but this is capped at £3,600 gross per annum (£2,880 net). Everyone in the UK between the ages 0 to 75 can make a pension contribution (and babies and children can have a pension plan too) and receive tax relief at 20%, 40%, or 45% depending on their tax rate.

Table 8.1 shows the net cost to an individual based on different rates of tax relief – the higher rate of tax, the more the individual receives in tax relief. The net cost of a gross contribution of £64 is £51 to a 20% taxpayer, £38 to a 40% taxpayer, but only £35 to a 45% taxpayer.

This favourable tax treatment means that average earners can expect to save money in taxes paid over their lifetime by contributing to a private pension plan rather than to a traditional savings account. This amount

**Table 8.1** *Pension and tax relief*

| Gross amount | Net cost to 20% taxpayer | Net cost to 40% taxpayer | Net cost to 45% taxpayer |
|---|---|---|---|
| £64 | £51 | £38 | £35 |
| £130 | £104 | £78 | £72 |
| £263 | £210 | £158 | £145 |
| £531 | £425 | £319 | £292 |
| £1,068 | £854 | £641 | £587 |

*Source:* Author's calculations

varies enormously, from 8% of the present value of all contributions (Sweden), to 24%–29% (Australia, Canada, Denmark, Switzerland, the UK, and the US) and around 50% (Israel, Lithuania, the Netherlands, and Mexico) (OECD, 2018, pp. 4–5).

Another significant benefit is the exemption from Income Tax, Capital Gains, and Inheritance Tax. There is no Income Tax on dividend/interest income from the investment, no capital gains tax, nor Inheritance Tax on pension funds. In the UK, assets over certain value (£325,000 for single and £650,000 for a couple) held outside pension funds are subject to 40% Inheritance Tax on death. However, pension funds are not normally subject to Inheritance Tax. These tax benefits enhance the appeal of saving in a pension fund.

## 8.7. Pension plans with most flexibility

There are three types of pensions in the UK: State Pension, occupational pensions, and personal pensions. Personal pensions are set up by individuals, and their key advantages are greater flexibility and investment choice. Unlike occupational pensions and State Pension, you can access money in a personal pension from the age of 55 (increasing to 57 from 6 April 2028) and enjoy a wider range of investments. In addition, a self-invested personal pension (known as a SIPP), a type of personal pension, allows individuals to buy commercial property as well as invest in stocks and shares. A personal pension can therefore provide a financial bridge for individuals who wish to retire before the age when they become eligible to State Pension, or an occupational pension.

## 8.8.  Trade-off between overpaying a mortgage and topping up a pension

When making a decision to overpay a mortgage or contribute to a pension, there are six factors to consider: age, tax bracket, mortgage rate, attitude to risk, general financial health, and existing pension provision. This chapter now discusses these factors in turn.

### 8.8.1.  Age

It is argued that there is an inverse relationship between age and pension contributions: the younger an individual, the greater the importance of a pension plan because compound interest can significantly enhance returns on contributions when time is on an individual's side. However, if you are less than 15 or 20 years from retirement, it is recommended that you focus on reducing your mortgage. Once the mortgage is paid off, you can then redirect as much of that money as you can into your pension plan.

We can demonstrate this using a simple example. Imagine that you have £250 of surplus income and you are debating whether to overpay on your mortgage or contribute to a pension. Assuming a 7% growth rate, Table 8.2 shows the benefit of investing when you are young.

This table shows that if you invest £250 per month at 7% return, you can accumulate a fund of £86,000 in ten years. However, this doubles every ten years. A longer timespan brings more significant benefits: a £250 monthly contribution grows to a fund of £172,000 after 20 years, £345,000 after 30 years, and nearly £700,000 after 40 years.

Table 8.2 *Saving early and compound interest*

| £250 monthly contribution | 40 years – starting at age 25 | 30 years – starting at 35 | 20 years – starting at 45 | 10 years – starting at 55 |
|---|---|---|---|---|
| Total contributions | £120,000 | £90,000 | £60,000 | £30,000 |
| Total value | £691,809 | £345,527 | £172,532 | £86,107 |
| Growth | £571,809 | £255,527 | £112,532 | £56,107 |
| Growth as % of total fund | 83% | 74% | 65% | 65% |

*Source:* Author's calculations

A longer investment period also means a higher percentage of the fund value comes from compound interest: growth accounts for 65% of the total value for ten to 20 years, but this rises to 74% for 30 years, and 83% for 40 years. The earlier you start, the more you can benefit from compound interest.

### 8.8.2. Tax bracket

Tax treatment increases the value of contributions in a pension plan. A pension plan offers tax relief (20%, 40%, 45%) on contributions and tax-free investment growth. This makes pension plans a great tax-saving strategy. However, mortgage payments do not receive tax relief but are made after income taxes are paid. Therefore, the same amount of money has a different value depending on how it is used.

This can be illustrated in table 8.3: paying £250 towards your mortgage requires £312 of gross income for a 20% taxpayer, £416 for a 40% taxpayer, and £454 for a 45% taxpayer. However, if you wish to make a gross contribution of £250 into a pension plan, it only costs £200 to a 20% taxpayer, £150 to a 40% taxpayer, and £137.50 to a 45% taxpayer.

If you are in a high tax bracket, pension plans are a great tax-saving strategy, and making a maximum pension contribution may be desirable. When tax relief is combined with compound interest, the effects can be powerful, as illustrated in Table 8.4. Assuming a £250 net contribution into a pension, a 40% taxpayer accumulates more than £1.1 million after 40 years, £575,000 after 30 years, £287,000 after 20 years, and £143,000 after ten years. A 45% taxpayer builds an even bigger fund.

Table 8.3  *Net cost of pension contributions and tax rates*

|  | Paying off mortgage – gross cost | Paying into a pension – net cost | Difference |
|---|---|---|---|
| £250–20% tax rate | £312 | £200 | £112.50 |
| £250–40% tax rate | £416 | £150 | £266 |
| £250–45% tax rate | £454 | £137.50 | £316.50 |

*Source:* Author's calculations

**Table 8.4** *Value of pension contributions over different investment terms*

| £250 net monthly contribution | 40 years investing – starting at age 25 | 30 years investing – starting at 35 | 20 years investing – starting at 45 | 10 years investing– starting at 55 |
|---|---|---|---|---|
| 20% | £864,805 | £431,952 | £215,708 | £107,676 |
| 40% | £1,153,113 | £575,984 | £287,663 | £143,624 |
| 45% | £1,257,989 | £628,379 | £313,838 | £156,701 |

### 8.8.3. Mortgage rate

The question of whether to pay off your mortgage or top up your pension also depends on the mortgage rate. If your current mortgage rate is low, it might make more sense to invest in a pension plan, where you might be able to get a higher rate return. For example, if the mortgage rate is 1% and investment return is 7%, there is a 6% differential. If your mortgage rate is 1% and the investment return is 9%, there is an 8% difference, and so topping up your pension might become attractive.

However, if your mortgage rate is high, paying it down may save you more interest than you could generate from investments from your pension plan. For example, if your mortgage rate is 3%, it might be better to pay of your mortgage if your investment return can only give you 1–2% return. However, if the investment return was 5–9%, then it might become more attractive to invest.

### 8.8.4. Attitude to risk

When deciding between paying off a mortgage or topping up a pension, your attitude towards investment risk can significantly impact the choice made. Contributing to a pension often involves taking on some level of investment risk, which can vary depending on an individual's risk tolerance. A person with a lower risk tolerance is likely to opt for investments that offer lower returns, as they are more risk-averse. In such cases, it might be more advantageous to focus on paying off a mortgage rather than increasing pension contributions, as the potential returns from low-risk investments may not outweigh the benefits of reducing mortgage debt.

On the other hand, a higher risk taker is more comfortable with the possibility of fluctuating returns and may be willing to invest in higher-risk options, which can potentially yield higher returns. For these individuals, topping up their pensions might be a more suitable strategy, as the potential gains from high-risk investments could surpass the advantages of paying off their mortgage early. Ultimately, the decision between paying off a mortgage or increasing pension contributions is influenced by an individual's risk tolerance and financial goals, and it's essential to carefully consider both options in light of your personal circumstances.

## 8.9. Case studies

### 8.9.1. Pension to pay off mortgage

Beth, 55, is eligible to cash in a £150,000 pension from a previous employer, and she wonders whether she should use £100,000 to pay off her mortgage. In making this decision, there are several considerations to take into account:

a)  *Income in retirement*: The purpose of a pension is to provide an income in retirement. If an individual takes money from their pension to pay off their mortgage, they need to work out what income they will have when they stop working.

b)  *Early repayment charge*: It is advisable to check whether there are any penalties or charges for paying off the mortgage early or paying more than 10% of the mortgage balance.

c)  *Fluctuating pension values*: If the value of a pension has been fluctuating, cashing in means that an individual will not have a chance to see the recovery of the fund.

d)  *Income tax implications*: Cashing in a defined contribution pension pot has tax implications. Up to 25% can be taken as a tax-free lump sum, and the remainder will be treated as taxable income in the tax year in which the borrower takes it.

e)  *Limit on future contributions*: Cashing in a defined contribution pension reduces the amount an individual and employer can pay into a pension in the future.

### 8.9.2. Paying into a pension or paying off mortgage

A man is debating whether to contribute more into his pension or pay off his mortgage. Mo, 58, is an additional taxpayer earning £150,000

**Table 8.5** *Pension contribution and tax saving for a 45% taxpayer*

|  | Current | Proposed |
|---|---|---|
| **Annual pension contribution** | £24,000 | £60,000 |
| **Tax relief** | £10,800 (£54,000 over 5 years) | £27,000 (£135,000 over 5 years) |

per annum and owns a house worth £850,000 with £200,000 out-standing mortgage with his wife. Their monthly payment is £2,000, and they would like to clear their mortgage in five years and retire debt-free at 63.

He pays £24,000 a year into his defined contribution pension, and his wife is not currently contributing into a pension, but she has a pension pot of £45,000. They arrived in the UK in 2005 and have not yet made enough National Insurance Contributions to qualify for the full state pension (requiring 35 years of National Insurance contributions). They are also debating whether they could get better returns by investing in the stock market. They have £650,000 in investments and savings and a £130,000 property abroad. In addition to their mortgage payments, they spend £2,500 a month on outgoings and a further £6,000 a year on holidays.

There are two possible ways to optimise Mo's finances. First, he could optimise his pension by increasing the current level of contribution to its maximum limit as this will offer substantial tax savings, as outlined in Table 8.5.

Second, they could pay off their mortgage now using their investments. This would enable them to save £2,000 per month in mortgage payments, which could be redirected into a pension or other tax-efficient vehicles.

The couple has options, and the decision they take depends on their attitude to risk and debt.

### 8.9.3. The High Income Child Benefit Charge

The High Income Child Benefit Charge applies to people who get Child Benefit and whose income (or partner's income) exceeds a certain threshold. The charge is 1% of the amount of Child Benefit received for every £100 of excess income.

Pension contributions can be used to reduce the High Income Child Benefit Charge, because the income (includes earnings, dividends, savings income, P11d benefits like company car) used by HM Revenue and Customs to calculate the charge is 'adjusted net income'. Any pension contributions made by an individual will reduce their adjusted net income. If this is sufficient to bring it below threshold, the charge will be reduced or avoided (Grant, 2023).

### 8.9.4. Reclaiming personal allowance

Pension contributions can also be used to reclaim the personal allowance when your income exceeds £100,000. For every £2 of income over £100,000, an individual loses £1 of their personal allowance until they have no allowance left. This makes the effective rate of tax 60% (40% tax on the £2 and 40% tax on the lost £1) on income between £100,000 and £125,140 (Pru, 2023).

### 8.9.5. Mitigate against capital gains tax

Pension contributions are also used to mitigate against Capital Gains Tax (Pru, 2023). An individual's basic rate band is increased by the amount of any grossed up personal pension contribution. For example, Jim's earnings are £50,270 per year. He has just sold his buy-to-let property and, after his CGT allowances, has a taxable gain of £10,000, throwing him into the higher rate tax band.

Whilst his income is within the basic rate band, the Capital Gain (after allowances) from the sale of his property falls into the higher rate band. He therefore decides to make a personal pension contribution of £8,000 net (£10,000 gross). This means that his basic rate band is increased by £10,000, and his Capital Gain now fits within his basic rate band. As a result, he pays Capital Gains Tax at a lower rate, in addition to the tax relief, he receives on his pension.

## 8.10. Conclusion

Paying into a pension plan gives an individual the benefit of tax relief. The top-up contributions from tax relief enhance the returns from a pension. However, a pension plan is designed to provide an income in retirement and using it to pay off a mortgage has several disadvantages.

First, the borrower has to wait until 55 (this will increase to 57 in 2028) before they can take benefits from their personal pension and potentially later from occupational pensions. This means that this is not a suitable vehicle for someone who wishes to pay off the mortgage much earlier. Second, only 25% is tax-free, and the remainder amount will be heavily taxed if taken in one go. Third, using the pension fund to pay off a mortgage, the individual is moving money from a tax-efficient environment into a taxable environment (e.g. inheritance tax). As we live longer, it is imperative to save and invest for retirement and to start this process early to take advantage of compound interest. Our desire to pay off our mortgage quickly needs to be balanced against this goal.

## References

Amromin, G., Huang, J., and Sialm, C. (2007). The tradeoff between mortgage prepayments and tax-deferred retirement savings. *Journal of Public Economics*, 91, 2014–2040. Available at: https://faculty.mccombs.utexas.edu/clemens.sialm/amromin_huang_sialm07.pdf [Accessed 12 July 2023].

Bond, J., and Doonan, D. (2020). The growing burden of retirement rising costs and more risk increase uncertainty. *National Institute on Retirement Security*. Available at: www.nirsonline.org/wp-content/uploads/2020/09/The-Growing-Burden-of-Retirement.pdf [Accessed 12 July 2023].

Department for Work and Pensions. (2023). State pension age review 2023. Available at: www.gov.uk/government/publications/state-pension-age-review-2023-government-report/state-pension-age-review-2023#:~:text=The%20government%20accepted%20the%20recommendation,the%20latest%20life%20expectancy%20projections [Accessed 12 July 2023].

Dunstan, T. (2022). Almost a third of savers to rely on state pension as primary retirement income. *Pensionsage*. Available at: www.pensionsage.com/pa/Almost-a-third-of-savers-to-rely-on-state-pension-as-primary-retirement-income.php#:~:text=The%20research%2C%20which%20included%20a,source%20of%20income%20in%20retirement [Accessed 12 July 2023].

Fidelity Investments. (2023). How much do I need to retire? Available at: www.fidelity.com/viewpoints/retirement/how-much-do-i-need-to-retire#:~:text=Key%20takeaways,are%20ways%20to%20catch%20up [Accessed 12 July 2023].

Grant, J. (2023). Child benefit – can you avoid the tax charge? *Royal London*. Available at: https://adviser.royallondon.com/technical-central/pensions/state-benefits-pension-manuals/child-benefit-avoiding-the-tax-charge/ [Accessed 12 July 2023].

OECD. (2018). Financial incentives and retirement savings. Available at: www.oecd. org/daf/fin/private-pensions/Financial-Incentives-and-Retirement-Savings-2018-highlights.pdf [Accessed 12 July 2023].

OECD. (2023). Pensions at a Glance 2021. Available at: www.oecd-ilibrary.org/sites/ ca401ebd-en/1/3/3/5/index.html?itemId=/content/publication/ca401ebd-en&_csp_=9d37797bd84847326841f27f588be463&itemIGO=oecd&itemContent Type=book [Accessed 12 July 2023].

Office for Budget Responsibility. (2023). Welfare spending: Pensioner benefits. Available at: https://obr.uk/forecasts-in-depth/tax-by-tax-spend-by-spend/welfare-spend-ing-pensioner-benefits/#:~:text=Pensioner%20benefit%20spending%20in%20 2023,5.3%20per%20cent%20of%20GDP [Accessed 12 July 2023].

ONS. (2020). Living longer: Changes in housing tenure over time. Available at: www.ons.gov.uk/peoplepopulationandcommunity/birthsdeathsandmarriages/ ageing/articles/livinglonger/changesinhousingtenureovertime [Accessed 12 July 2023].

ONS. (2022). Economic labour market status of individuals aged 50 and over, trends over time. Available at: www.gov.uk/government/statistics/economic-labour-market-status-of-individuals-aged-50-and-over-trends-over-time-september-2022/ economic-labour-market-status-of-individuals-aged-50-and-over-trends-over-time-september-2022 [Accessed 12 July 2023].

ONS. (2022a). Reasons for workers aged over 50 years leaving employment since the start of the coronavirus pandemic: Wave 2. Available at: www.ons.gov.uk/employment andlabourmarket/peopleinwork/employmentandemployeetypes/articles/reasonsfor workersagedover50yearsleavingemploymentsincethestartofthecoronavirus pandemic/wave2 [Accessed 12 July 2023].

Pensions Policy Institute. (2017). 'General election 2017 state pension age rises' PPI briefing note number 97. Available at: www.pensionspolicyinstitute.org.uk/ media/1365/201706-bn97-general-election-2017-state-pension-age-rises.pdf [Accessed 12 July 2023].

Phoenix. (2023). Over 50s driven out of work due to ill health have just 5% of the wealth of those retiring early by choice. Available at: www.thephoenixgroup.com/ newsroom/news/over-50s-driven-out-work-due-ill-health-have-just-5-wealth-those-retiring-early [Accessed 12 July 2023].

Pru. (2023). Pension contributions can be a valuable tool in an individual's tax planning. Available at: www.mandg.com/pru/adviser/en-gb/insights-events/insights-library/ pension-tax-planning?utm_source=legacyurls&utm_medium=301&utm_ campaign=/knowledge-literature/knowledge-library/pension-tax-planning/ [Accessed 12 July 2023].

Retirement Income Journal. (2022). You'll need 11 times final salary to retire on: Aon Hewitt (30 June 2022 Issue). Available at: https://retirementincomejournal.com/article/ youll-need-11-times-final-salary-to-retire-on-aon-hewitt/ [Accessed 12 July 2023].

Retirement Living Standards. (2023). Picture your future. Available at: www.retirement livingstandards.org.uk/ [Accessed 12 July 2023].

World Economic Forum. (2017). We'll live to 100 – how can we afford it? Available at: https://www3.weforum.org/docs/WEF_White_Paper_We_Will_Live_to_100.pdf [Accessed 12 July 2023].

World Economic Forum. (2019). Investing in (and for) our future. Available at: https://www3.weforum.org/docs/WEF_Investing_in_our_Future_report_2019.pdf [Accessed 12 July 2023].

## Chapter Nine
## Developing a successful property portfolio

### 9.1. Introduction

The US is a nation with a highest number of landlords. It is reported that more than 10 million people receive rental income from 20.5 million rental housing units, with an average landlord has three properties and an annual rental income of $97,000 (Reed, 2023).

The UK is also a 'buy-to-let' nation, with landlords owning 4.8 million properties worth over £1.4 trillion. In 2020–2021, it was reported that there were 2.74 million landlords, but by 2023 Unbiased notes this had decreased to 2.65 million (ONS, 2022; Rickman, 2023). Private renting is the second most common type of accommodation in England, providing housing to 4.6 million people, or nearly a fifth of households (EHS, 2022). Buy-to-let mortgages were introduced in 1996 and took off from the 2000s onwards. Paragon, a specialist buy-to-let lender, estimates that there were over two million buy-to-let mortgages outstanding with a value of £279 billion in 2021, representing 18.1% of all mortgages outstanding (Paragon, 2021).

In Australia, there are 2.2 million private landlords (15% of households) who own 3.3 million residential properties (30% of the 11 million). They provide housing to more than 26% of households, or 2.9 million, who rent privately. The overwhelming majority of landlords (90%) in Australia

DOI: 10.4324/9781003297765-9

own one or two investment properties (Longview and Pexa, 2023, p. 4, 6; Forbes, 2023).

Robert G. Allen in *Creating Wealth* advocates using a property portfolio to accumulate wealth and retire in ten years (Allen, 2011). He suggests that we should aim to buy at least one property per year for ten years, and this should produce a net worth of $500,000 or $1 million based on two properties per year. A property portfolio refers to a collection of investment properties that you own. This can include buy-to-let properties, a holiday home, and commercial properties. This chapter examines the advantages and disadvantages of building a property portfolio as a strategy to build wealth.

## 9.2. Buy-to-let properties in the UK

House prices in the UK have increased rapidly since the late 1990s and early 2000s. With homes becoming unaffordable, many people rent instead of buy. Indeed, in 2000 only 10% of all homes in England were privately rented, but this had more than doubled by 2017, to 20.3%. The English Housing Survey shows that the proportion has decreased slightly, with 4.6 million, or 19% of households, renting privately in 2021–2022 (EHS, 2022).

Evidence suggests that a typical landlord in the UK is not a professional one; many landlords use rental income as supplementary. The Ministry of Housing, Communities and Local Government (MHCLG) commissions the English Private Landlord Survey (EPLS) to inform government of the characteristics and experiences of landlords and how they acquire, let, manage, and maintain privately rented accommodation. The survey in 2021 provides interesting insights into the profile of landlords in the UK (English Private Landlord Survey, 2022; see also Scanlon and Whitehead, 2016):

- **Reasons for becoming landlords**: Five percent let property as a full-time business, and 95% are part-time landlords. They invest in property because they prefer property to other investments (42%) and see buy-to-let property as a vehicle to provide a retirement income (40%).
- **Basis of ownership**: Ninety-four percent let property as an individual or group of individuals, 5% as part of a company, and 1% using other structures.

- **Number of properties**: Forty-three percent of landlords have one rental property (providing 20% of private rented housing), 39% own two to four properties (providing 31% of private rented housing), and 18% own five or more properties (45% of private rented housing).
- **Age**: Almost two-thirds (63%) are aged 55 or older, and a third (35%) are retired. This suggests that many landlords have owned properties for a long time and benefited from capital growth. Indeed, the survey shows that 53% has been in business for 11 years or more. This shows that much property wealth is held by the older generations.
- **Ethnicity**: Eighty-eight percent of landlords identified as white, 4% Indian, 2% Black, 1% Pakistani or Bangladeshi, and 5% Other.
- **Gender**: Fifty-five percent of landlords are male, 44% female, 1% identified as Other. Female landlords are more likely than male landlords to own only one property, while male landlords are likely to own two or more properties.

## 9.3. Why do some people prefer buy-to-let properties as investments?

When looking to invest our money, we look for several attributes: liquidity, hedge against inflation, stable growth rates, ability to leverage, good tax shelter, steady cash flow, and portable. Unfortunately, there are no investments that could give us all of these qualities. However, Allen (2011) argues that finding an investment that is stable (steadily increasing in value) and powerful (using leverage to produce wealth-producing rates of return) can give us the key to wealth accumulation. He believes that property qualifies as a powerful and stable investment.

Property is widely perceived to be an attractive investment for several reasons. First, property provides capital growth potential, and the performance of property prices supports this belief. In 1980, an average property in the UK cost £20,000, but this rose to £58,000 by 1990, £270,000 by 2021, and £304,000 in March 2023, representing a staggering 1,520% nominal increase or 15 times more expensive than in 1980 (Open Access Government, 2022).

In 2021, Savills predicted that the average house price would increase by 21.1% between 2021–2025 (5.25% annual increase) (Crane, 2021a). This is comparable to pre-COVID, as Shawbrook reports that the average buy-to-let property price increased by 5.6% per annum to £258,900 between 2019 and 2020 (Shawbrook Bank, 2021, p. 14).

Assuming a 5% annual increase, the Table 9.1 shows the increase in property value in ten, 20, and 30 years. A property costing £100,000 today would be worth £163,000 in ten years (63% increase), £265,000 in 20 years (265% increase), and £430,000 in 30 years (430% increase). A £250,000 property today would be worth £407,000 in ten years (63% increase), £663,000 in 20 years (65% increase), and more than £1 million in 30 years (400% increase).

Property values, however, do not go up in a straight line. Property prices fell during the financial crisis (2008), then moved in a zigzag fashion between 2010–2013, before experiencing a further steady growth until 2022 when prices started to drop due to surging mortgage interest rates. This decline is forecasted to be temporary, and house prices are expected to recover. (Partington, 2022).

A second advantage of investing in buy-to-let property is a steady stream of income in the form of rent. The EPLS survey shows that the average gross rental income (before tax and other deductions) grew by 15% between 2018 and 2021, from £15,000 to £17,200, with the percentage earning less than £20,000 falling, and those earning more than £20,000 increasing, as can be seen in Table 9.2.

A UK lender, Foundation Home Loans, carried out a survey of around 900 landlords in 2021 and found that in Q1 2021, the typical portfolio was worth around £1.2 million and generated an annual gross rental income of £54,000. Based on an average portfolio size of 7.3 properties, the typical property value was £168,000, generating an annual income of around £7,397 per property, or £616 per calendar month. This represents a yield of 4.4%. The profile of a typical portfolio remains largely unchanged, with terraced houses the most commonly owned type of rental property (Foundation Home Loans, 2021). The pandemic changed tenant preferences, and semi-detached properties became more popular as tenants wanted more space. A survey by

Table 9.1 *Growth of property prices based on 5% increase*

| Property price | 10 years | 20 years | 30 years |
|----------------|----------|----------|----------|
| £100,000 | £163,000 | £265,000 | £430,000 |
| £200,000 | £325,000 | £530,000 | £864,000 |
| £250,000 | £407000 | £663,000 | £1 million |

*Source:* Author's calculations

Shawbrook Bank in 2021 shows that the top three priorities for tenants looking for their next rental property were having a garden (48%), the size/number of bedrooms (40%), and having off-street parking (26%) (Shawbrook Bank, 2021, p. 7).

Research also shows that buy-to-let properties generate a good return for landlords. A survey by Hamptons International shows that 84% of landlords who sold up made pre-tax profits. In 2020, the average landlord sold their property for £78,000 more than they paid for it, or a 42% return on their investments. After deductions, they achieved a net profit of £43,340. However, this excludes rental income. Adding capital gains and rental income together gave the average landlord a total net profit of £76,820, representing a 39% return on their investments, or an annual yield of 4.3% (Holborn Assets, 2021). On average, landlords had owned their properties for around 9.1 years.

There are huge regional variations in capital gains enjoyed by landlords across England and Wales. In 2019, for example, those in London are reported to make an average pre-tax gain of £253,850 from their properties – the highest gains were seen in Kensington & Chelsea, where investors achieved an average of £924,010 more than they had paid for them. Buy-to-let landlords in the north-east, on the other hand, made an average pre-tax gain of £11,710 (Harvey, 2020).

However, rising mortgage rates and rental reforms (e.g. mortgage interest tax relief) have made buy-to-let investing less attractive and encouraged many landlords to sell their properties. Hadi Khalisadar, a landlord with 150 properties and has his own lettings agency, told *The Guardian* newspaper in February 2023 that 20% of the landlords he worked with wanted to sell and "lots of landlords are very anxious, to the extent that some are saying they cannot afford their properties." He believes lettings are now "over-regulated", and rising interest rates have not helped. Smaller landlords appear to be more affected, with one

Table 9.2 *Average gross rental income of landlords in the UK*

|  | 2018 | 2021 |
| --- | --- | --- |
| <£20,000 | 61% | 56% |
| £20,000–£49,999 | 26% | 29% |
| £50,000 or more | 13% | 15% |
| Median | £15,000 | £17,200 |

*Source:* EPLS (2018, 2021)

confessing: "It causes me huge amounts of stress and anxiety. We have a big mortgage and, on top of that, an outlay every month to cover the expenses." (Marsh, 2023).

A third attraction of property as an investment is the ability to leverage, which can magnify returns. Leverage refers to the use of borrowed money (mortgage debt) to finance the purchase of a property with the expectation that the income or capital gain from the new asset will exceed the cost of borrowing.

Imagine that you are looking to buy a property worth £100,000 and you put down 25% (£25,000) and borrow 75% of the value (£75,000). If the property goes up by 10% to £110,000, you'll make a 40% profit on your initial investment of £25,000 (£110,000 less £75,000=£35,000; £10,000 gain); if the property goes up by 20% to £120,000, you'll make £45,000 or 80% gain.

In a falling property market, the losses are also magnified – a 10% fall in the property value represents a 40% loss on your investments, 20% fall in 80% loss. Landlords still have to service the debt, which, if the property has a void period at the same time, would exacerbate the loss even more. In a rising market, leverage can magnify returns, but in a falling market this can magnify losses. This can be seen in Table 9.3.

Now, imagine that instead of investing in a property, you use £25,000 to invest in some stock in ABC Ltd at £10 per share. With £25,000, you can acquire 2,500 shares. If the share price increases by 10% to £11, you have made a profit of £2,500 or achieved 10% return on your original capital. Without leverage, you therefore achieve the same rate of return as the market.

A fourth advantage of owning buy-to-let properties is that it provides a source of passive/residual income. Passive/residual income is a regular income you get that may require your effort, determination, and time at the beginning. It is different from active income because it does not

Table 9.3 *Effects of leverage*

| Property value | 10% fall | 20% fall | 10% rise | 20% rise |
|---|---|---|---|---|
| £100,000 with 75% mortgage and 25% own money | 40% loss | 80% loss | 40% gain | 80% gain |
| £200,000 with 75% mortgage and 25% own money | 40% loss | 80% loss | 40% gain | 80% gain |

*Source:* Author's calculations

require you to work continuously to earn money. It can operate independently of you. For these reasons, unlike earned income, you can have multiple sources of income and own several properties, if you have the ability to obtain the funds needed to pay for them. This can give you financial independence and time freedom, because you do not need to work to earn money to pay for your expenses. As we have seen earlier, some landlords in the UK earn a gross rental income of £54,000 per year. If their expenses are lower, they have enough money to cover their expenses and so are financially independent.

In addition to the financial aspects, an important appeal of property is control. When you invest in a property, you, in effect, become your own fund manager – you can decide what to do with the investment, how to enhance its value, who to let the property to, and how much rent to charge. In addition, property is a tangible asset, and you can see it, use it, enjoy it, and show it off.

Investing in stocks and shares, on the other hand, normally requires relinquishing control to someone else, and you can lose money. For example, 300,000 investors in Neil Woodford's failed funds experienced high financial losses as well as emotional anguish– in 2020 they were told that they would only receive 48 to 58p per share in comparison with the 100p price they had paid at launch five years earlier. By 2023, investors were only able to recover approximately 77p to the pound (Collinson, 2020; Makortoff, 2023).

Investing in buy-to-let properties brings several disadvantages. First, the costs of acquiring a property are high. For example, individuals need a 25% deposit and pay a 3% surcharge in stamp duty on additional properties, such as second homes and buy-to-let properties. This means that buying a £250,000 property requires a minimum capital outlay of £62,500 of deposit and £10,000 in stamp duty, plus legal and valuation fees.

Second, since 2017, renting has become less profitable due to tax changes to interest payments. Previously, landlords were able to deduct interest costs before paying tax. This effectively gave higher-rate taxpayers 40% tax relief on their mortgage payments. Now, landlords will be given a flat-rate tax credit based on 20% of their mortgage interest. This won't have a negative impact on most landlords who were already basic-rate taxpayers but will mostly affect those who are higher or top-rate taxpayers. However, one problem is that landlords will have to declare the gross income on their tax return (under the old system, they could declare rental income after deducting mortgage repayments). This could change the tax status of some individuals, moving from a basic to a higher rate, which would mean a higher tax bill. This affects the yield on buy-to-let property. In addition, landlords also face increased regulation. For example, energy efficiency improvement requirements (Energy Performance Certificate) impose further expense without necessarily being able to increase rents to cover the cost.

Third, buy-to-let properties are not seen as tax efficient. Changes in mortgage interest relief means that some landlords will pay more Income Tax than before, and many landlords have seen their profits significantly reduce – in particular, higher and additional rate taxpayers.

Here's an example of how their tax has changed for a landlord paying £500 a month in mortgage interest and receiving £1,000 a month in rent. There is no change for a basic rate taxpayer, but a higher-rate taxpayer has to pay more tax (50% more in this example), as can be seen in Table 9.4.

Buy-to-let properties are also not tax efficient in other ways – for example, the rate of Capital Gains Tax is higher than the rate charged on gains made on shares and stocks. Unlike pensions, they are also subject to Inheritance Tax at 40%.

Fourth, there is a lack of diversification. Owning buy-to-let properties, in addition to your main home, means that your investments are concentrated in property. Over-concentration carries its own risks, including interest-rate rises, fluctuating property prices, illiquidity, tying your personal fortunes to the global and national economies, and to factors beyond your control. For example, you may find it difficult to sell a property as a result of a recession, due to growing unemployment, and stringent mortgage lending criteria. As a result, you may not be able to liquidate your assets and get hold of money you need to achieve your goals (e.g. retire, make home improvements, and pay Inheritance Tax).

**Table 9.4** *Changes in treatment of mortgage interest*

| Income tax calculations | Before 2017 | From 2020 |
|---|---|---|
| Annual rental income | £12,000 | £12,000 |
| Annual mortgage interest | £6,000 | £6,000 |
| Taxable annual income | £6,000 | £12,000 |
| Tax credit for mortgage interest | 0% | 20% (£1,200) |
| Tax bill (basic rate) | £1,200 | £1,200 |
| Tax bill (higher rate) | £2,400 | £3,600 |

One example can demonstrate this point. A man died leaving behind an estate worth £1.5 million, with a large proportion in properties. His children had to pay Inheritance Tax within six months, but falling property prices made it difficult for them to get a mortgage to raise the necessary funds to pay the Inheritance Tax.

The golden era for buy-to-let landlords is believed to have come to an end in September 2022, as higher mortgage rates, greater regulation, and financially stretched tenants make the future tough for landlords. A survey of landlords in early 2023 shows that nearly 45% of landlords plan to sell (Finbri, 2023).

### 9.3.1. House in multiple occupancy (HMO)

Landlords have been looking for a better business model and have shifted to house in multiple occupancy (HMO) letting – in 2021, it was reported that 15% of landlords in the UK owned an HMO. A survey by Paragon in 2022 showed that 22% of HMO landlords sought to buy more already-converted HMOs, 20% planned to acquire properties to convert into HMOs, 8% planned to sell them, 4% to sell all HMOs, and 53% did not plan to change their portfolio (Paragon, 2022, p. 10).

HMO properties have become more lucrative than standard single let rental properties, particularly in UK cities with a significant student and young professional population. For example, renting a five-bed property in Cambridge to a single family is likely to achieve £3,000 per month. However, renting out this property as an HMO could fetch £4,500 per month instead of £3,000, with each tenant paying £900. More tenants means a higher gross rental income and a higher annual yield (Patania, 2022). The average yield for a HMO is reported to be 7.6% (Paragon, 2022, p. 11).

Research by Paragon shows that 46% of HMO tenants are young single people, with 47% being students and 41% white collar, clerical or professional workers. However, these groups tend to be mobile, and so many do not stay for long. The majority of tenancies are for one year (54% one year and 12% less than a year), 20% for two years, and only 2% last longer than five years (Paragon, 2022, p. 11).

### 9.3.2. Furnished holiday lettings

Furnished holiday lettings also offer another way to make money from a property. A holiday let mortgage is designed for people looking to borrow money to buy a property that will be let out on a short-term basis to tourists as a business. It differs from a holiday home mortgage, where you borrow money to buy a second home that only you will use. It is also different from a buy-to-let mortgage, where you borrow money to buy a property that will be let out on a long-term basis.

There are three tax advantages of this type of letting: the ability to deduct mortgage payments from income before Income Tax is calculated, classification of income as 'relevant earnings' allowing you to make tax-advantaged contributions to your pension, and Capital Gains Tax relief. The property is treated as a trading asset (whereas buy-to-let rent is treated as investment income) and is potentially eligible for Business Asset Disposal Relief when sold, where owners pay a lower rate of Capital Gains Tax. In 2019–2020, 2,000 taxpayers owning furnished holiday lettings claimed Business Asset Disposal Relief on gains of £366 million, saving between £30 million and £65 million of tax (OTS, 2022, p. 57).

However, furnished holiday lettings are not popular. According to the Office of Tax Simplification, there were 127,000 furnished holiday lettings businesses in 2019–2020, forming only 4.5% of the 2.8 million UK properties owned by individuals. The majority of furnished holiday lettings are in the UK (87.4%), and around 13% in EEA, such as France and Spain (OTS, 2022, pp. 62, 94–95).

There are several possible reasons for the lower popularity of furnished holiday lettings. First, rental income can be uncertain as occupancy is quite seasonal and there might be long void periods. There is also less choice with holiday let mortgage products (400 in January 2023, in comparison to 2,400 for buy-to-let (Springall, 2023), mortgage interest rate is higher, a minimum income is required (£10,000–£40,000 in addition to rental income), and a bigger deposit is necessary (25%–30%) (Soye, 2023). In addition, losses cannot be offset against other taxable income. This type of letting also does not offer a stable source of income and requires more upkeep such as cleaning.

### 9.3.3. Serviced accommodation

Serviced accommodation has also become popular with landlords and property investors in recent years. This offers fully furnished, self-contained accommodation with hotel-style services included, and is a type of short-term letting serving different markets, including tourists and leisure travellers, business people, contractors, and others.

There are several possible advantages of investing in serviced accommodation, including higher rental income (a property let on a long-term contract at £750 per month could potentially achieve £750 per week as a short-term let), possible tax benefits (serviced accommodation counts as furnished holiday let, which means that mortgage interest can be claimed as a tax allowance), and more lenient tenancy laws and regulations (guests have no security of tenure and are easy to evict). However, serviced accommodation requires a large initial capital outlay and housekeeping services. In addition, there are restrictions from lenders and local councils on short-term lets (Property Investments UK, 2023).

### 9.3.4. Owning properties via a company structure

Individuals can buy properties via a company structure, known as incorporating, which allows them to benefit from more attractive tax rates. Between 2016 (when tax relief reductions for landlords were introduced) and 2020, the numbers of companies set up rose by more than 128%. By the end of 2020, there were nearly 290,000 buy-to-let companies set up – 34% are in London and the south-east. While EPLS 2021 shows that only 4% of landlords own properties via company structure, research by Foundation Home Loans indicates that, while the majority of landlords rent their property as an individual (80%), 18% of landlords now hold at least one of their properties within a limited company structure (Foundation Homeloans, 2021).

According to a survey by the Office of Tax Simplification in 2022, there are several perceived benefits of owning a property in a company structure, including desire for limited liability, ability to exercise control over when income is taken out (the potential to allow rental profits to accumulate), desire for flexibility over transfer of ownership of the shares (e.g. succession planning across generations of a family), tax benefits (Corporation Tax starts at 19% in comparison to Income Tax of 20%, 40%, and 45%), and the ability to deduct interest costs. However, there are also tax disincentives to use a company structure, including the second layer of tax (when individuals have to pay dividend tax when income is withdrawn) (OTS, 2022, pp. 37–38).

Incorporation also incurs additional costs as investors need to have a separate tax return for the limited company, available mortgage products are more limited, and interest rates are higher. Although the number of mortgage products for limited companies has increased since 2017, this is still lower than the number available to individuals.

## 9.4. Raising capital

Raising the cash to get started is often the biggest hurdle. The costs can be pretty hefty and usually fall into two key categories: the initial buying costs and the ongoing day-to-day expenses. Firstly, let's talk about the costs you will face when you're buying the property. This includes the deposit, which is a chunk of the property's price that you have to pay upfront. Then there is the stamp duty, which is basically a tax you pay when you buy a property. Don't forget about the valuation fee for assessing how much the property is worth, the legal fees for all the paperwork, and a fee your lender charges for setting up the mortgage.

Once you have bought the property, you are not done spending yet. Now come the running costs. If you are hiring a letting agent to take care of things, you'll need to fork out for their fees. You will also have to keep up with your mortgage interest payments. Insurance is another must-have, covering everything from the building itself to any contents and even missed rental payments. You are also responsible for annual checks like gas safety inspections. And don't forget about getting an electrical certificate, plus budgeting for regular maintenance and those unexpected repairs that always seem to pop up at the worst time.

The biggest costs are the deposit and stamp duty costs. To buy a property worth £200,000 to let out, you normally need a 25% deposit or more (depending on rental income), and money to pay stamp duty (if this is your second property you will incur a 3% surcharge). To raise the capital, there are several options, including the following:

### 9.4.1. Saving

One of the most straightforward ways to raise capital for property investment is through disciplined saving. This involves setting aside a portion of your income regularly and accumulating it over time until you have enough funds to invest. To speed up the process, consider creating a dedicated savings account, automating deposits, and looking for ways to cut expenses or increase your income. Additionally, you can explore high-interest savings accounts or short-term investment vehicles to grow your savings more quickly while ensuring the funds remain relatively accessible when needed.

### 9.4.2. Remortgage

If your property has risen in value – because you've improved it or the market has gone up – you can withdraw that equity by borrowing against the new value. However, the amount you can take out will be capped by either the property's rental value (if you're taking out a new buy-to-let loan on your rental property) or your own income (if you're borrowing against your main home). Also, watch your cash flow, as more debt means higher interest payments. If you barely break even or make a monthly loss, you won't be able to ride out problems and sustain mortgage payments. Lastly, watch out for hefty repayment penalties from your current lender.

### 9.4.3. Sell

This is a good option if your property is not meeting your goals anymore, but selling may land you with a big Capital Gains Tax bill, unless it is your main residence.

### 9.4.4. Pension

Under current rules, those over 55 can withdraw all, or part, of their pension pot and use the money as they please – including on a buy-to-let. In a poll by YouGov for insurer Royal London, three in ten people aged between 45 and 54 said they were considering accessing their retirement funds to purchase a buy-to-let property. Royal London says that such a move can be an expensive mistake. It calculates that, on a £400,000 pension, savers would need to pay £120,000 in Income Tax if they withdrew the full amount as one lump sum. There is also stamp duty to pay on the purchase – £12,300 stamp duty on a £310,000 property, bringing the total cost to £132,300. The estate agency Hamptons International estimates it would then take them six and a half years to earn their money back on a buy-to-let. This estimate is based on house price growth of 1.24% a year and a rental yield of 6%. It doesn't take into account the various costs of being a landlord, such as repairs, maintenance, and void periods (Maunder, 2019). Using a withdrawal from a pension to buy residential property is not tax efficient because individuals have to pay Income Tax when they take money out of their pension fund.

A more tax-efficient strategy is to keep money in a pension fund and use it to buy a property. This would allow them to enjoy the tax benefits associated with a pension fund. However, pension funds in the UK can only buy commercial property, not residential or buy-to-let. Buying a commercial property through a pension fund is increasingly popular amongst small business owners who choose to buy their business premises through their pension scheme. For example, Bill runs a family business with his wife. The business was initially run from the family home. However, due to expansion, the family decides to move to a business premise. Bill buys the premise within his Self Invested Personal Pension (SIPP). As his fund was not sufficient to buy the property outright, he borrows 30% of the purchase price. The property is owned by the SIPP and is let to the company for a rent of £12,000 per annum. The rent is deductible from the business' profits and paid into the SIPP (owned by Bill). The rent is tax-free in the SIPP. The rent paid into the SIPP helps to build up its value. If the SIPP decides to sell the property, there is no Capital Gains Tax to pay (Bradford, 2011). In addition, pensions are also not subject to Inheritance Tax. In short, buying a commercial property using a pension fund is more tax efficient as there is no Income Tax, Capital Gains, and Inheritance Tax.

### 9.4.5. Joint venture

Team up with a family member or friend who has the cash, ideally in the form of a loan on which you offer them a fixed interest rate. You could split the profits, with them putting up the money and you doing the work, or you could both put in equal amounts and share the rewards. No matter how close you are, always draw up a declaration of trust that says who will invest how much, who will do which tasks, and which property it is secured on. Also state what happens if things go well – and if they don't.

### 9.5. Strategies with minimal risks

In the preceding section, we discussed building a property portfolio to accumulate wealth. However, this approach may not be suitable for everyone due to the costs, risks, and complexity. The following section therefore examines two simpler ways: renting out a room and downsizing.

### 9.5.1. Rent-a-room

One simple way to increase income is to let out a spare room in your house to a lodger and receive tax-free income through the Rent a Room Scheme to overpay a mortgage. This scheme was introduced in 1992 to alleviate the shortage of rental accommodation and give homeowners a tax-free income (up to a limit) if they rent out a fully furnished room in their main home.

The Rent a Room Scheme has been more popular since the economic crisis of 2008 for several reasons. First, economic uncertainty encourages many households to look for a 'side hustle' to give them another stream of income by turning a spare room into extra cash. Between 2008–2009 and 2019, for example, the value of tax relief through the Rent a Room Scheme has more than trebled, increasing from £45 million to £140 million (Magnus, 2021).

Second, the proliferation of technology platforms (e.g. *www.gumtree. com*, *www.easyroommate.co.uk*; *www.spareroom.co.uk*, and *www.rightmove. co.uk*) have made it easier, quicker, and simpler to advertise a spare room. These websites have been designed to simplify the process of listing and advertising spare rooms, making it more accessible for everyone. They provide intuitive interfaces and tools that allow homeowners to create detailed listings complete with photographs, descriptions, and other pertinent information about the space available.

Third, if homeowners do not like having a lodger full-time, they could consider fractional letting to people who need a place to stay during the weekdays using websites such as *www.mondaytofriday.com*. They also could choose to rent to foreign students for a few weeks at a time, or to tourists through sites such as airbnb.com or booking.com, enabling them to meet different people normally for a few nights at a time.

Fourth, the increase in the tax-free amount from the Rent a Room Scheme has enhanced its attractiveness. The allowance started with £3,250 in 1992, increasing to £4,250 by 1997, but this rose to £7,500 from April 2016. This enhanced tax-free allowance not only provides a financial incentive for homeowners to participate in the scheme but also makes the prospect of renting out a room more financially viable.

Spare Room estimates that there are around 21 million empty spare rooms in homes in England alone, and only 2% of homeowners rent out their spare rooms (Hutchinson, 2022). Indeed, it is reported that 38%

of homes (9.4 million) in England are under-occupied with two or more spare rooms (Lewis, 2022).

The potential rental income from these spare rooms is enormous. In 2013, *The Independent* reported that 1.7 million homeowners had a lodger, generating £3.3 billion of rental income per year, which covered 27% of mortgage payments (Johnson, 2013). If all the approximately 13.7 million spare bedrooms in 2013 were rented out, it was calculated that this could potentially generate £5.8 billion a month or around £69 billion a year (Hampshire Chronicle, 2013). If this calculation is correct, then renting out 21 million spare rooms could generate more than £105 billion of rental income. In terms of capital value, it was estimated in 2022 that these spare rooms were worth £791 billion, with the average value of £42,000 per room. The value of each room in London was calculated at £76,000 in comparison to £54,000 for the south-east and £22,000 for north-east (Hutchinson, 2022).

*The Guardian* reports that the cost of living crisis has encouraged many households to take in a lodger to help pay bills, with visitors to the site Monday to Friday increasing by 30% in the 3 months leading to November 2022. SpareRoom expects many more homeowners to take in lodgers (Whateley, 2022). However, a survey by the Office of Tax Simplification (OTS) published in 2022 shows that only a small percentage (13%) of homeowners are using the Rent a Room Scheme, nearly 80% of those surveyed had not used it, 4.9% had used it but no longer qualified, and 2.7% no longer wanted to use it. Of the 13.1% who used the scheme, nearly 46% earned more than £7,500 and so had to pay tax, and more than 50% earned less than £7,500, and so no additional tax was payable (OTS, 2022, p. 96).

Some homeowners have successfully used the Rent a Room Scheme to pay off their mortgage early. Simon came to the UK from Poland in 2005 and was renting a room for three years, paying on average £400 per month. When his girlfriend joined him in 2008, they rented a one-bed house at the cost of £650 per month. Like many Polish people, their dream was to own their own place, but they did not think it was possible. However, after receiving encouragement that the dream was within their reach, they decided to plan their purchase. Their first step was to save as much money as they could by moving in with another couple. They rented a four-bed house with another Polish couple for £900 and took in two lodgers. This rental income enabled them to save for a first house deposit. In 2010, they bought a four-bedroom house for £155,000 and paid a 10% deposit. Their monthly mortgage was £1,000, but they received £1,100 per month by renting out three rooms. After seven years, they had saved enough to buy another property for £130,000, renting it out for £850 per month. In March 2023, they were able to repay their mortgage on their main residence and achieve mortgage-free status after 13 years.

Some homeowners take in lodgers for social reasons. One landlord, 64 years old, has taken in 15 lodgers over 25 years and describes it as "a lovely arrangement". She charges £65 a week and says that it is really easy to do her tax return as she just needs to tick 'Rent a Room Scheme' box. She explains the reasons why she likes the scheme: "Back when I was at university I enjoyed sharing flats, so when I bought my first house I thought it would be nice to have someone to share the bills with. It also meant I wasn't coming home to an empty house" (Forrest, 2014).

Many single people find renting a room the most convenient and simple form of tenancy. Most room lets include all bills in the weekly rent, and the house is likely to be well looked after with a live-in landlord. More importantly, they do not need to pay a huge deposit as many live-in landlords are happy to accept a one-week deposit. They also do not need to sign a long contract, giving them much greater flexibility if their circumstances change. One lodger, 33, rents a room in north London after splitting up with a girlfriend because it is simpler, without requiring to pay a large deposit, sign a 12-month tenancy agreement, and deal with a lot of bills. The average age of a lodger is reported to be 31 years old, with a fifth aged between 36 and 50 (Forrest, 2014).

The Rent a Room Scheme is designed for homeowners to take in one lodger with no Capital Gains Tax implication when they come to sell the property. However, if homeowners rent to more than one lodger, HMRC regard this as using parts of their home to run a lettings business, and so there will be Capital Gains Tax implication.

### 9.5.2. Downsizing

Downsizing to a smaller property or buying a cheaper one could enable you to repay the mortgage early. If you live in a three-, four, five-bedroom family home and your children are grown and have moved out, downsizing to a smaller house will save money on your mortgage payments and running costs.

One couple bought a house in 2007 for £195,000 and took out a £150,000 mortgage. In 2020, the house was worth £330,000 with £96,000 remaining on the mortgage. They plan to buy another property by the coast for £250,000. Assuming they sell their property for £330,000 and after clearing their £96,000 mortgage, they would have £234,000 to put towards their new property and legal and estate agents' fees. The fees are estimated at £7,000, giving them a net amount of £227,000 to spend on their new house. However, the purchase of the new property incurs many costs, including stamp duty, and so a few thousands need to be allowed for these. Assuming these additional costs amount to £5,000, the homeowners would have £222,000 for the new property and may need to borrow £28,000. By downsizing, they reduce their mortgage by two-thirds, from £96,000 to £28,000 (Wallis, 2020).

Some people downsize due to a change in personal circumstances. Edward used to own a four-bed detached house with his wife worth £475,000. When they got divorced, they sold their marital home to buy two small flats costing £200,000 each, enabling them to be mortgage free.

However, downsizing is not very popular. A survey of 2,000 people shows that only a fifth of people plan to downsize in their retirement, another 38% said they would not and 42% were unsure. The most cited reason (28%) why the respondents do not want to downsize is due to strong attachment to their home. In addition, there are also financial considerations that influence the decision – one in ten didn't believe they would make enough money from downsizing, while almost a quarter said it would be too expensive. Indeed, the average cost of moving homes in the UK is around £12,000 (for legal fees, stamp duty, surveyor costs, estate agent fees, and removal costs) (Crane, 2021b).

Londoners are the most likely to want to downsize, with 39% having plans to do so in their retirement, compared to 16% of residents in the south-east (Crane, 2021b). Homeowners in London are likely to make significant gains when they sell their property, especially if they have been in their property for a long time, as prices have increased rapidly. John, for example, sold his two-bed flat in Surrey for £435,000 in 2017 and paid off his £225,000 mortgage (interest only). He moved to the Lake District and rented for six months at a cost of £500 per month while he was looking for a suitable property. He bought a three-bedroom detached house in the Western Lake District with half an acre of land for £265,000. The property was originally on the market for £290,000, but he was able to negotiate a £25,000 discount as he was a cash buyer with no requirement for a mortgage. He used the proceeds from the sale of his flat and his ISA to pay for the new house.

Bill owned a three-bed semi-detached house in London for which he paid £149,000. In 2018, he sold it for £775,000 and bought a five-bed detached house in Leicester for £550,000. The move to a city outside London enabled him to live in a bigger property with a surplus fund. This reduced financial pressures on him and enabled him to leave his 9-to-5 job to become a freelance consultant and spend more time with his wife.

## 9.6. Other ways to make money from property

There are several ways to make money from your home, besides taking in a lodger, including the following (Meyer, 2022):

a) **Rent out your driveway or parking space**
   Your driveway could be rented out to drivers to earn extra income, especially if the property is near a station or a popular venue. This could be advertised on websites such as YourParkingSpace, Just-Park, Park On My Drive. ParkLet is an option for longer-term lets.
b) **Rent a loft or garage space for storage**
   Homeowners could rent out their garage or loft space for storage using Storemates (detailing the location, size, and monthly cost) or spareground.co.uk to advertise the space. It is estimated that you can earn about £1,000 a year on average from renting an unused garage or loft space.
c) **Rent your home for filming**
   Every film and TV drama needs suitable set locations, and you can advertise your home on agency websites such as Scouty, Location Works, Amazing Space, Shootfactory, or Lavish Locations for a spacious family home. It is reported that hosts can make £500 to £2,000 a month (from one to three bookings) by renting out their home as a location. The average shoot length is one day.
d) **Rent out your spare room to a home worker**
   Many people now work from home, but many do not have the space to set up a home office. If you have a spare room, it is believed that you could earn extra money by renting it out to a home worker. Achievable income depends on your location and your property.

## 9.7. Conclusion

In this chapter, we discussed the benefits and drawbacks of utilising a buy-to-let portfolio as a means to grow wealth and different ways of making money from property. By taking a comprehensive look at these aspects, readers can better understand the potential risks and rewards associated with property investment, enabling you to make informed decisions and craft a tailored approach to building your property portfolio. We also looked at two additional strategies of taking the rent-a-room approach and downsizing your living space to enhance your financial stability and potentially expedite your mortgage payoff.

By delving into these strategies, our goal is to equip you with a thorough understanding of the various options at your disposal, empowering you to make well-informed decisions that align with your financial objectives and personal situation. Ultimately, adopting the right strategies can pave the way for a more secure and prosperous financial future.

## References

Allen, R. (2011). *Creating Wealth: Retire in 10 Years Using Allen's Seven Principles.* New York: Free Press.

Bradford, S. (2011). Buying commercial property through a pension fund. *Taxinsider.* Available at: www.taxinsider.co.uk/buying-commercial-property-through-a-pension-fund [Accessed 15 July 2023].

Collinson, P. (2020). Neil Woodford investors take hefty loss as payouts begin. *Guardian*, 28 January. Available at: www.theguardian.com/business/2020/jan/28/neil-woodford-investors-loss-payouts [Accessed 15 July 2023].

Crane, H. (2021a). House prices to see £10,000 average increase this year, says heavily revised forecast – and one region is predicted to SURGE 30% by 2025. *Thisismoney.* Available at: www.thisismoney.co.uk/money/mortgageshome/article-9338495/What-happen-house-prices-2021-Savills-predicts-4-growth.html [Accessed 15 July 2023].

Crane, H. (2021b). Staying put: Only a FIFTH want to downsize when they retire, with most saying they are 'too attached' to their current home. *ThisIsMoney*, 12 November. Available at: https://www.thisismoney.co.uk/money/mortgageshome/article-10182025/Only-20-want-downsize-attached-homes.html [Accessed 15 July 2023].

English Housing Survey. (2022). English Housing Survey 2021–22: Headline report. Available at: www.gov.uk/government/statistics/english-housing-survey-2021-to-2022-headline-report/english-housing-survey-2021-to-2022-headline-report [Accessed 15 July 2023].

English Private Landlord Survey. (2018). Department for levelling up, housing and communities. Available at: https://assets.publishing.service.gov.uk/government/

uploads/system/uploads/attachment_data/file/775002/EPLS_main_report.pdf [Accessed 15 July 2023].

English Private Landlord Survey. (2022). Department for levelling up, housing and communities. Available at: https://assets.publishing.service.gov.uk/government/uploads/system/uploads/attachment_data/file/1078643/EPLS_Headline_Report_2021.pdf [Accessed 15 July 2023].

Finbri. (2023). UK Landlords' report 2023. Available at: www.finbri.co.uk/blog/uk-landlords-report-2023 [Accessed 15 July 2023].

Forbes, K. (2023). How many Australians own an investment property? Available at: https://propertyupdate.com.au/how-many-australians-own-an-investment-property/#:~:text=Note%3A%20That%20means%20that%20around,investors%20hold%201%20investment%20property [Accessed 15 July 2023].

Forrest, A. (2014). More homeowners open their doors to lodgers. *Guardian*, 26 August. Available at: https://www.theguardian.com/money/2014/aug/16/more-homeowners-open-their-doors-to-lodgers [Accessed 15 July 2023].

Foundation Homeloans. (2021). Buy to let landscape 2021 – latest portfolio size and yield report. Available at: https://www-uat.foundationforintermediaries.co.uk/news/buy-to-let-landscape-2021-latest-portfolio-size-and-yield-report/ [Accessed 15 July 2023].

Hampshire Chronicle. (2013). Letting out spare rooms could net £69 bn. Available at: https://www.hampshirechronicle.co.uk/news/10464589.letting-spare-rooms-net-69bn/ [Accessed 15 July 2023].

Harvey, E. (2020). Landlords made over £78,100 in buy-to-let sales 2019. Available at: www.buyassociationgroup.com/en-gb/2020/06/17/landlords-made-over-78000-on-buy-to-let-sales-in-2019/ [Accessed 15 July 2023].

Holborn Assets. (2021). Should you consider a buy-to-let investment in 2021? Available at: https://holbornassets.com/blog/mortgage-property/buy-to-let-investments-in-2021/ [Accessed 15 July 2023].

Hutchinson, M. (2022). Why the rental market is (currently) screwed? *SpareRoom*, 6 October. Available at: https://blog.spareroom.co.uk/why-the-rental-market-is-screwed/ [Accessed 15 July 2023].

Johnson, A. (2013). Renting out spare rooms earns homeowners more than £3.3 billion of rental income per year. *The Independent*, 8 November. Available at: https://www.independent.co.uk/property/renting-out-spare-rooms-earns-homeowners-more-than-ps3-billion-a-year-8929462.html [Accessed 15 July 2023].

Lewis, D. (2022). Waste of space – Homeowners sitting on £791.5bn in spare room value. *Introducer Today*. Available at: https://www.introducertoday.co.uk/breaking-news/2022/1/waste-of-space--homeowners-sitting-on-791-5bn-in-spare-room-value?source=newsticker [Accessed 15 July 2023].

Longview and Pexa. (2023). Private renting in Australia – a broken system. Available at: https://longview.com.au/hubfs/Private-renting-in-Australia-a-broken-system-LongView-PEXA-Whitepaper.pdf [Accessed 15 July 2023].

Magnus, E. (2021). Britons saved £140m in taxes when renting out spare rooms last year: Could you take advantage of the Government's Rent a Room Scheme?

*ThisIsMoney*, 22 May. Available at: https://www.thisismoney.co.uk/money/buytolet/article-9601661/Britons-renting-spare-rooms-saved-140m-taxes-using-Government-scheme.html [Accessed 15 July 2023].

Makortoff, K. (2023). Woodford fund compensation likely to total 77p in the pound. *Guardian*, 20 April. Available at: www.theguardian.com/business/2023/apr/20/woodford-fund-compensation-for-investors-likely-to-total-77p-in-the-pound#:~:-text=Woodford%20fund%20compensation%20for%20investors%20likely%20to%-20total%2077p%20in%20the%20pound,-This%20article%20is&text=The%20administrator%20of%20the%20failed,their%20savings%20after%20its%20collapsed [Accessed 15 July 2023].

Marsh, S. (2023). 'Lots of us are very anxious': Why Britain's buy-to-let landlords are selling. *Guardian*, 24 February. Available at: www.theguardian.com/money/2023/feb/24/lots-of-us-are-very-anxious-why-britains-buy-to-let-landlords-are-selling [Accessed 15 July 2023].

Maunder, S. (2019). Should you invest your pension pot in a buy-to-let property? *Which*. Available at: www.which.co.uk/news/article/should-you-invest-your-pension-pot-in-a-buy-to-let-property-aTgkf3A6Rk3x [Accessed 15 July 2023].

Meyer, H. (2022). Six ways to make money from your home. *Guardian*, 5 September. Available at: https://www.theguardian.com/money/2022/sep/05/ways-to-make-money-from-your-home-lodger-parking-space [Accessed 15 July 2023].

Office of Tax Simplification. (2022). Property income review: Simplifying income tax for residential landlords. Available at: https://assets.publishing.service.gov.uk/government/uploads/system/uploads/attachment_data/file/1113149/OTS_Property_Income_review.pdf [Accessed 15 July 2023].

ONS. (2022). Property rental income statistics: 2022. Available at: www.gov.uk/government/statistics/property-rental-income-statistics-2022/property-rental-income-statistics-2022 [Accessed 15 July 2023].

Open Access Government. (2022). UK house prices are 65 times higher today than in 1970. Available at: www.openaccessgovernment.org/uk-house-prices-are-65-times-higher-today-than-in-1970/138813/ [Accessed 15 July 2023].

Paragon. (2021). 25 years of buy-to-let. Available at: www.paragonbank.co.uk/resources/paragonbank/documents/mortgages/buy-to-let/25-years-of-btl-report [Accessed 15 July 2023].

Paragon. (2022). The HMO report. Available at: www.paragonbankinggroup.co.uk/pCMS_BO/Resources/paragon-group/documents/reports-presentations/2022/changing-face-of-hmos [Accessed 15 July 2023].

Partington, S. (2022). House price predictions for the next five years and how to protect yourself from drops. *Ideal Home*. Available at: www.idealhome.co.uk/house-manual/house-price-predictions-for-the-next-five-years [Accessed 15 July 2023].

Patania, G. (2022). Benefits of HMO property investment. Available at: https://hmo-architect.com/blog/about-hmos/benefits-of-hmo-property-investment [Accessed 15 July 2023].

Property Investments UK. (2023). Investing in serviced accommodation: A comprehensive guide. Available at: www.propertyinvestmentsuk.co.uk/serviced-accommodation/ [Accessed 15 July 2023].

Reed, C. (2023). 35 insightful landlord statistics. Available at: https://getflex.com/blog/landlord-statistics/ [Accessed 15 July 2023].

Rickman, C. (2023). What does the future hold for buy to let? *Unbiased*. Available at: www.unbiased.co.uk/discover/mortgages-property/buy-to-let-renting/what-does-the-future-hold-for-buy-to-let [Accessed 15 July 2023].

Scanlon, K., and Whitehead, C. (2016). The profile of UK private landlords, Council of Mortgage Lenders. Available at: www.lse.ac.uk/business/consulting/assets/documents/The-Profile-of-UK-Private-Landlords.pdf [Accessed 15 July 2023].

Shawbrook Bank. (2021). The changing face of buy-to-let. Available at: www.shawbrook.co.uk/media/4170/b2b-btlreport-20210820.pdf [Accessed 15 July 2023].

Soye, A. (2023). Holiday let mortgage criteria – top tips. Available at: www.holidaycottagemortgages.co.uk/holiday-let-mortgage-criteria-you-need-to-be-aware-of/ [Accessed 15 July 2023].

Springall, R. (2023). Buy to let choice recovers from market turmoil. *Moneyfacts*. Available at: www.moneyfactsgroup.co.uk/media-centre/consumer/buy-to-let-choice-recovers-from-market-turmoil/#:~:text=%E2%80%9CIt%20is%20encouraging%20to%20see,slowly%20dipped%20below%20this%20level [Accessed 15 July 2023].

Wallis, V. (2020). Should we pay off the £96,000 left on our mortgage when downsizing? *Guardian*, 23 November. Available at: https://www.theguardian.com/money/2020/nov/23/should-we-pay-off-the-96000-left-on-our-mortgage-when-downsizing [Accessed 15 July 2023].

Whateley, L. (2022). Cost of living crisis: Could taking in a lodger help you pay your bills? *Guardian*, 19 November. Available at: https://www.theguardian.com/business/2022/nov/19/cost-of-living-crisis-lodger-bills-renting-out-room-home [Accessed 15 July 2023].

## Chapter Ten
## Successful property ownership
### The final consideration

### 10.1. Introduction

Homeownership can confer significant psychological, emotional, and financial benefits, but often this requires us to take on a substantial amount of debt. Successful homeownership involves not only a careful choice of property but also effective mortgage management. In this concluding chapter, we aim to guide you through the crucial decision-making process of choosing a property and managing your mortgage.

### 10.2. Purchasing the ideal property type

Choosing the right property is a critical step in successful homeownership. A well-chosen property not only retains its value, regardless of market fluctuations, but it also safeguards you from the risks of negative equity. Finding the ideal property requires extensive research into the attributes that contribute to its desirability. These attributes directly affect the property's pricing and its potential for resale in the future. In my previous book *Buying Your Home*, I provide a useful framework called the 7Ss (Luu and Tonthat, 2021):

DOI: 10.4324/9781003297765-10

## 10.2.1. Safety

Opt for an area where people feel secure. Safety is a primary concern when choosing a property. Living in a safe neighbourhood not only provides peace of mind for you and your family but also significantly impacts the value of your property. A secure environment is often characterised by low crime rates, well-lit streets, active neighbourhood watch programmes, and the presence of security systems in homes. These factors collectively contribute to a sense of safety and security among residents. When people feel safe in an area, they are more likely to invest in properties there, driving up demand and, consequently, property values. Moreover, a safe neighbourhood tends to attract long-term residents, creating a stable community that further increases the area's appeal. Additionally, safety has a direct correlation with the quality of life. It allows residents to freely engage in outdoor activities, fosters stronger community bonds, and promotes overall well-being.

## 10.2.2. Spaciousness

A spacious property in a neighbourhood with ample public open spaces can significantly enhance living standards and appeal to potential buyers. A spacious property not only provides comfort and flexibility for the current residents but also holds significant appeal for potential buyers in the future. A spacious home allows for more natural light, better ventilation, and room for customisation according to personal preferences. It offers the freedom to design your living space as per your needs, whether it's creating a home office, setting up a play area for children, or a garden room.

## 10.2.3. Schools

Proximity to reputable schools is a considerable advantage, especially for families with children, as it directly impacts their education and future prospects. Living close to good schools provides children with easy access to quality education. It eliminates long commutes, giving children more time for extracurricular activities, homework, and rest. This can have a positive effect on their overall academic performance and well-being. Properties near good schools often maintain or increase their value over time. As demand for such properties remains high, they can offer excellent resale value. Potential buyers, especially those planning to start or grow a family, often prioritise such locations, making these properties an attractive investment.

### 10.2.4. Supermarkets

Easy access to supermarkets offers convenience and potentially improves the quality of life for the residents. The proximity of supermarkets also contributes to healthier living. With a variety of fresh produce readily available, residents are more likely to incorporate these nutritious foods into their diet. This easy access can foster better eating habits and contribute to overall well-being. Properties located near supermarkets tend to have higher property value due to the desirability and convenience they offer. This could be a significant consideration for homeowners or potential property investors.

### 10.2.5. Stations

Properties close to stations (railway or tube) provide convenience, save on transportation costs, and are often sought after in the resale market. Living near a station means shorter commutes to work, school, or other activities. This proximity can save residents considerable time daily, which adds up significantly over weeks and months. It also eliminates the stress and uncertainty of traffic jams or road closures affecting travel times. The convenience factor, coupled with the potential savings on transportation, make these properties attractive to a wide pool of potential buyers. This demand can drive up property values and ensure a better return on investment for homeowners.

### 10.2.6. Sports and stadiums

Being near a sports venue or football stadium can offer opportunities for additional income through renting out driveway/parking space. On game days or during sporting events, there's often a high demand for short-term rentals from fans travelling to watch the event. Homeowners can take advantage of this by renting out their property or spare rooms.

### 10.2.7. Special features

Being close to facilities like a hospital, university, pub, or natural elements like the sea or a pleasant view can greatly enhance the property's value and desirability. Proximity to these features can significantly increase a property's value and desirability. Hospitals and universities provide convenience for professionals and stimulate local economies, while pubs and restaurants enhance the local nightlife. Natural features like the sea and views offer aesthetic and recreational appeal, and green spaces contribute to overall quality of life.

## 10.3. Mortgage security

After identifying a desirable property, the next priority is to ensure that a mortgage commitment can always be met.

### 10.3.1. Ability to meet monthly mortgage obligations

A key reason why many people cannot pay their mortgage is a fall in income or a rise in expenditure, due to changes in interest rates, household income and expenses (e.g. sudden rise in expenses, loss of income due to unemployment, illness), and personal circumstances (e.g. illness, bereavement, or divorce). To build your financial resilience, it is imperative to adopt the following principles, known as 'PIE'. This principle will enable you to build a solid financial foundation to withstand financial challenges, but you also need to have a plan to pay off your mortgage. This requires you to have a repayment mortgage in place, an overpayment strategy, and regular review.

### 10.3.2. Planning for the future

Taking out a mortgage requires planning ahead. One crucial aspect to consider is the age when you are looking to retire as this affects the term of the mortgage. For example, if you are aged 30 and looking to stop or reduce work by 55, then the term needs to be around 25 years or less. If you are aged 35 and plan to retire by 55, then the term needs to be 20 years or less. A second issue to consider is whether the mortgage you take on is affordable now and in the future. In ensuring that it is affordable, it is important to ensure that the cost of all debt payments (mortgage and all credit commitments) do not constitute above 30% of your income. Budgeting and adopting financial discipline are also essential, as this enables you to live within your means, avoid overspending and getting into debt, save money, build a financial buffer, and achieve financial resilience.

### 10.3.3. Income protection policy

Illness, especially long-term, can drain any amount of money you may have. An income protection policy is highly recommended as this will provide you with a replacement income in the event of ill health. Taking out such an insurance policy enables you to transfer your personal risks to an insurance company and gives you peace of mind.

### 10.3.4. Emergency fund

Having an emergency fund is critical because it provides you with a financial buffer to deal with any emergencies, such as boiler or car break-down, leaks, repairs, or a rise in mortgage payments as a consequence of a change in interest rates. Financial advisers generally recommend holding enough money sufficient to cover at least three to six months of expenses. However, the amount required might be higher (six to 12 months or so) if you do not have stable employment or a guaranteed income.

## 10.4.  Key actions to pay off a mortgage

There are three crucial aspects to ensure paying off your mortgage: opt for a repayment mortgage, have an overpayment strategy, and monitor your mortgage. A repayment mortgage is a common type of loan where both the principal and the interest are paid off over a fixed term. An overpayment strategy is a method where you pay more than your regular monthly mortgage payment whenever possible, which can help reduce the overall interest and shorten the loan term. Lastly, consistently monitoring your mortgage will allow you to stay informed about your loan status, track interest rates, and make timely decisions. Understanding these concepts is key to effectively managing your mortgage and potentially saving money in the long run.

### 10.4.1. Repayment mortgage

To ensure you'll pay off your mortgage, it is important to have a repayment mortgage, where you pay off the capital as well as the interest. This is the first step towards paying off the debt.

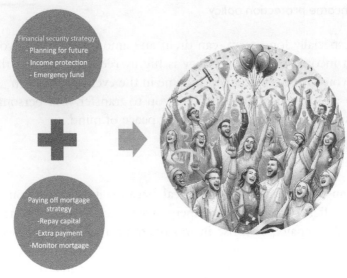

**Figure 10.1** *Successful property ownership roadmap*

### 10.4.2. Overpayment strategy

It is advisable to aim for a mortgage term that pays off your mortgage by the time you reach 50, as this allows you to concentrate on retirement planning. Make a commitment to overpay your mortgage, however small. You can set a weekly, monthly, or yearly goal. Perhaps you can start with a realistic amount (e.g. £25–£50 per month) and gradually increase as your income goes up (e.g. £100–£150). Lenders, for example, allow individuals with a tie-in deal (e.g. fixed-rate mortgage) to overpay 10% of their mortgage balance per year. If you overpay up to 10% per year, you can repay your mortgage within ten years; if you overpay by 9%, you can repay within 11 years and so on (Table 10.1). Choose a percentage of overpayment that suits your lifestyle.

### 10.4.3. Monitoring your mortgage

It is imperative to monitor and review your mortgage costs and your expenses regularly to ensure you can take advantage of any emerging opportunities. For example, you might spot that your fixed mortgage interest rate is coming to an end. Your regular review will enable you to put a new deal in place without slipping onto a potentially more expensive

Table 10.1 *Percentage of overpayment and the length of time to repay mortgage*

| % of overpayment | 10% | 9% | 8% | 7% | 6% | 5% | 4% | 3% | 2% | 1% |
|---|---|---|---|---|---|---|---|---|---|---|
| Years to pay off | 10 years | 11 years | 12 years | 13 years | 14 years | 15 years | 16 years | 17 years | 18 years | 19 years |

standard variable rate. Knowing when your deal ends also allows you to shop around for good deals before the expiry of your deal. Lenders allow homeowners to secure a new rate three to six months before the expiry of their current one.

## 10.5. Leveraging mobile apps to assist with mortgage repayment management

There are many apps out there that can you help budget, save, invest, and manage your money. Try out these apps and use them to accelerate the achievement of your goal of paying off your mortgage early.

## 10.6. The art of handling your money wisely

George Clason's book, *The Richest Man in Babylon*, provides valuable insights into financial management. He presents five key principles that can guide individuals in their journey towards better money management and financial stability (Clason, 2021).

### 10.6.1. Cultivate a habit of saving

One of the core tenets of financial wisdom is to save consistently. Clason recommends setting aside at least 10% of your income. These savings act as a safety net during unexpected financial emergencies. It's about creating a cushion that can support you when unexpected expenses arise.

### 10.6.2. Exercise control over expenditure

A fundamental rule in personal finance is to ensure that your spending is always less than your income. This strategy prevents debt accumulation and allows for surplus income that can be further invested to grow wealth. Effective budgeting and conscious spending are key to achieving this.

### 10.6.3. Transform your home into a profitable investment

For most individuals, their home represents a significant portion of their wealth. As such, it's crucial to make wise decisions regarding homeownership. Whether it's regular maintenance to preserve property value or potential upgrades to enhance its worth, treating your home as an investment can pay off in the long run.

### 10.6.4. Secure a future income stream

Unforeseen circumstances such as illness can drastically impact your earning capacity. Therefore, it's crucial to have measures in place to provide a future income stream. This could be through insurance policies or investments that yield regular returns, ensuring financial stability even during challenging times.

### 10.6.5. Enhance your earning potential

With inflation, the cost of living tends to rise over time. To maintain a comfortable lifestyle, it's important to ensure that your earnings keep pace with, or exceed, these price increases. Continuous learning and professional development can significantly enhance your earning potential over time. By investing in your skills and knowledge, you are investing in your financial future.

## 10.7. Conclusion

Taking on a mortgage to buy a house can be daunting due to the significant financial risks involved. One such risk is the potential decrease in the property's value, leading to negative equity when you try to sell. Unsold properties can become financial burdens, costing you money over time. For instance, an acquaintance of the author had to relocate for a new job and put his flat up for sale. However, with scant interest from potential buyers, he had to continue paying the mortgage and bills for the unsold flat while also managing financial commitments for his new house. It took several years to sell the flat and at a price significantly lower than its purchase price. Despite this, he was relieved to finally be free of the financial strain.

Another potential risk is failing to keep up with your mortgage payments, which could result in the distressing experience of repossession, often accompanied by social stigma. We once encountered a couple facing this harrowing prospect on Christmas Eve. The husband was unable to work due to back pain, causing their family finances to spiral downwards. Missed mortgage payments negatively impacted their credit score, hindering their chances of securing a better mortgage deal or obtaining loans and credit for temporary relief. With the economy entering a recession and house prices falling, they couldn't raise funds using their property. After weeks of distress, they lost their home along with their 10% deposit and were forced to rent. Fortunately, the rent was cheaper than their mortgage payment. These daunting prospects can discourage some from buying a property. However, it's important to note that repossessions are relatively rare, and these risks can be managed effectively.

As we wrap up this chapter, it's clear that taking on a mortgage is a significant financial decision that requires careful consideration. A wise decision can bring wealth, financial security, and enjoyment, while a poor decision can result in financial losses, worries and stress. To help you make a big financial decision, it might be useful to speak to a financial planner or mortgage adviser. Remember, every decision pertaining to your finances has the potential to shape your life, so take your time, weigh your options, and choose wisely.

## References

Clason, G. (2008). *The Richest Man in Babylon*. Signetbook. New York.

Luu, L., and Tonthat, Q. (2021). *Buying Your Home: A Practical Guide for First Time Buyers*. Abingdon: Routledge.

# INDEX

*Note*: Page numbers in *italics* indicate figures, and page numbers in **bold** indicate tables in the text

## A

accident, sickness, and unemployment (ASU) policy 95
active investment 109–110; *see also* investment
additional occupational sick pay (OSP) 96
affordable mortgage 67–68
age groups 15, 72, 88, 111, 115, 117; compound interest 122–123; mortgage debt impact on 14; property 133; tenure of housing by *14; see also* demographic changes
anxiety 3, 19, 37, 91, 136
apps: cashback 65; money management skills 64–65; mortgage 82; mortgage repayment 161
attitude to risk 44, 106, 108, 124–125

## B

balance sheet *see* net worth statement
budget/budgeting 51, 61–63, **62**, 65
buildings insurance 97; *see also* life insurance
buy-to-let properties 143–144; preferred as investments 133–139; in UK 132–133

## C

capital gains tax 127, 138, 140, 144, 147
cashback apps 65
cheaper mortgage deals 75–76
children, help children with getting a mortgage 33–34
comfortable retirement income target 118
credit cards 51–52
credit score 43
critical illness policy 94–95

## D

debts 1; affecting stability of economy and financial system 3–4; effect on financial well-being 2; effect of inflation on 42; impact on age groups 14, *14;* outstanding 68; paying off 52, 54, 88, 105–106; as percentage of GDP 2, *2;* personal 11–17; ratio to property value 12; unsecured 43, 106
defined contribution pension 116–117
demographic changes 114; *see also* age groups
depositor protection schemes 64

discounted mortgages 71; advantages and disadvantages of **74**
discretionary budget 63; *see also* budget/ budgeting
divorce, impact on mortgage 15, 148, 158
downsizing 147–149
driveway/parking space, renting of 149

**E**

early mortgage paying off strategy 49–53; *see also* paying off
early repayment charge 125
earning potential, how to enhance 162
emergency fund 43, 104, 105, 106, 159
employment, insecurity in 2–3
employment and support allowance (ESA) 96–97
endowment mortgages 101–102
ethnicity, property ownership 133
expenditure, control over 161
expenditure statement 58–61, **59–60**

**F**

family income benefit (FIB) 90–91
family's well-being 91–95
fees 148; of apps 65; investments 109–110, **109**; mortgage product fees 75
Financial Conduct Authority (FCA) 18, 64, 72
financial discipline 81–82
financial goals 57
financial impact of premature death 89
financial plan, review and assess of 64
financial security 36–37; for family in premature death 37–38
Financial Services Compensation Scheme (FSCS) 64
financial stability 36–37
financial stress 2, 17–19; levels of 17–18, *18*
financial well-being 38–39, *39*, 57
fixed budget 63; *see also* budget/ budgeting

fixed-rate mortgages 70–71; advantages of **74**; disadvantages of 70, **74**
freelance work 53
funeral cost 89–90
furnished holiday lettings, property 139–140

**G**

gender and property ownership 133
goal maps 56
goals 64
goal setting 54–55; *see also* visual goal setting
Great Financial Crisis of 2007–2009 4
gross domestic product (GDP) 1–4, *2*, 10, 115

**H**

health 2–3; financial 57; hazards 91–92; homeownership and 9; mental 19–20, 31, 37, 86
health hazards 91–95
High Income Child Benefit Charge 126–127
home contents insurance 97–98
home equity *34*, 34–36
home for filming, renting of 149
homeowners 2–3; facing interest rate rise risk 28–30; financial stability and security after payment 36; financial stress 17–18; home equity access of 35; home reversion plan 16; life without mortgage debt 20; long life due to no mortgage debt 20; losing liquidity after debt payment 41; overpayment 78; pension saving of 33; Rent a Room Scheme 146–147; repay off mortgage in 10 years 28
homeownership 7–21, 155–162; access to supermarkets 157; emergency fund 159; financial stress 17–19, *18*; global ratio of 9–10, *10*; health and 9; household debts and 11–17; mortgage in 17–19; mortgage insomnia and 19–20;

mortgage security 158–159; paying off mortgage 159–161; personal debts and 11–17; popularity and importance of 8–9; proximity to public convenience areas 157–158; proximity to schools 156; psychological well-being of 19–20; purchasing of right property 155; property, global value of 10–11; secure environment for 156; spacious property 156; sports and stadiums 157; stations (railway or tube) 157; wise money handling 161–162
household budget 31–32
household debts 1, 11–17, 19–20; *see also* debts
house in multiple occupancy (HMO) 139

## I

impulsive spending, avoidance of 52
income 52–53; amount required for retirement 116–118, *117*; estimation for budget calculation 61; in retirement 125; securing future stream 162; usage of other income for repayment 78–79
income-generating assets 53
income protection policy 92–94, 159
income statement 58–61, **59–60**
income tax **108**, 110, 121, 125, **138**, 143
individual savings account (ISA) 110–111
inflation 42, **43**
interest, length of 29, *29*
interest, saving of 27–28
interest-only mortgages 31, 69–70, 103
interest rate rise risk 28–30, 32
interest rates: higher in fixed-rate mortgage 70; inflation and 42; mortgage **108**
invest lump sum 104–106
investment returns 81, 103, 108, 124
investments 64, 101–111; active and passive approaches to 109–110; endowment mortgages 101–102; factors affecting decision to invest or pay off mortgage 107–108;

importance of fees in 109; in income-generating assets 53; individual savings account (ISA) 110–111; in self 53; in stocks and shares ISAs, borrower 105; trade-off between investing and paying off mortgage 106–107; transforming home into profitable 162; ways for early repay off mortgages 102–106; *see also* spending
invest monthly savings 103

## J

job insecurity 3
joint mortgage sole proprietor (JMSP) 33
joint venture 144

## L

landlords 131–141, **135**, 147
life choices 38
life insurance 90–91; defined 88; types of 90–91, *93*
lifetime tracker mortgages 71
limit on future contributions 125
liquidity 41–42
loans, size of 80–81
loft/garage, renting of 149
long-term financial goals 54
lower interest rate product 80–82
low savings in UK 95–96
lump sum term assurance 90

## M

management, mortgage 67–83; affordable mortgage 67–68; cheaper deal 75–76; faster rate of pay off mortgage 76–78; product fees 75; types of mortgages 70–74; ways of mortgage repayment 68–70, 78–82
measurable goal setting 55
mental imagery 55, 56
minimal risks, strategies to pay off mortgage 144–149

minimum income target 118
moderate income target 118
money management skills 49–66;
    apps use for 64–65; budget/
    budgeting 61–63; early mortgage
    payoff strategy 49–53; expenditure
    statement 58–61, **59–60**; financial
    plan, review and assess of 64; income
    statement 58–61, **59–60**; net worth
    statement 57–58; personal financial
    plan 53–57; spending and saving,
    documentation of 63; *see also* paying
    off; repayment
monitoring mortgage 160–161
monthly obligations 158
mortgage contracts 2; length of 3;
    payment/repayment of 3, 7;
    penalties 44
mortgage insomnia 19–20
mortgage payment protection insurance
    (MPPI) 95
mortgage prisoners 30–31, 73
mortgage rates 30, 40, 42, 44, 108; buy-
    to-let investing 135; in overpayment
    124; regular reviewing of 79–80
mortgage security 158–159
mortgage success 86–87

N

net worth statement 54, 57–58
no negative equity guarantee (NNEG) 16

O

occupational pensions 115–116, 121
off-setting 41, 73–74; advantages of 74;
    borrower 105; disadvantages of 74;
    pay off mortgage 78
opportunity cost of paying off mortgage
    early 39–40
overall financial situation, borrower 104
overpayment 43–44, 78; 10%
    overpayment 104, 105 age and
    overpayment 122–123; monthly
    overpayment 78; mortgage rates
    124; paying off 43–44; strategy 160;

tax 123; topping up pension and
    122–125; *see also* repayment
ownership 132; *see also* homeownership

P

passive investment 109–110
paying off 27–44, 125–126, 159–161;
    advantages of 27–39; disadvantages
    of 39–43; expensive debts
    105, 106; faster rate of 76–78;
    overpayment/repayment 43–44; into
    a pension 125–126; *see also* money
    management skills
'pay yourself first' approach 61
Penalties, early repayment 44
pensions 33, 121, 127–128; contributions
    43–44, 105; defined contribution
    pension 116–117; fluctuating values
    125; funds 143–144; occupational
    pensions 115–116, 121for paying
    off mortgage 125–126; self-
    invested personal pension (SIPP)
    121, 144; state pension *119*; State
    Pension age (SPA) 114; for tax relief
    120–121, **121**; trade off between
    mortgage overpayment and pension
    contributions 122–125; type of 121;
    *see also* retirement
permanent health insurance *see* income
    protection policy
personal allowance 127
personal debts 11–17; *see also* debts
personal financial plan 53–57
personal sacrifices in paying off mortgage
    early 40–41
premature death: impact on financial
    security for family 37–38; risks of
    88–89
private savings: importance of 118;
    required amount to be saved per
    month 119
product fees 75
progress of a financial plan 64; tracking
    55, 56, 57
property 131–150; buying properties via
    company structure 141; furnished
    holiday lettings 139–140; growth

in value 134; house in multiple occupancy (HMO) 139; letting with minimal risks 144–149; protection of property 97–98; raising capital 142–144; selling, property 143; serviced accommodation 140–141; ways to make money from 149; *see also* buy-to-let properties
protection, borrower 104, 105, 106; *see also* wealth protection
protection insurance 43
protection of property 97–98
psychological distress 17, 20
psychological well-being 19–20

**Q**

quality of life, and mortgage, 2, 21, 36, 40, 116, 156–158

**R**

raising capital, property 142–144
real estate, value of global property 10–11
relevant goal setting 55
remortgage 143
Rent a Room Scheme 145–147
renting, homeownership and *10*
repayment 43–44, 159; financial benefits of 28; ways of 68–70, 78–82; *see also* money management skills; paying off
reputation, of app developing company 65
retirement: importance of planning 114–116; income required for 116–118, *117*; saving for 32–33; *see also* pensions
reverse mortgage 16, 35
reviewing mortgage options, borrower 104
risks 44; attitude to 106; minimal risk strategies to pay off mortgage 144–149; of becoming mortgage prisoners 30–31; of premature death 88–89; reduction techniques 86–87

rounding up apps 65; *see also* apps, money management skills

**S**

sacrifices, personal 40–41
salary increase 52–53
saving 142, 161; debt-free homeownership and socially acceptable saving goal 113; interest payments 27–28; for retirement 32–33; tracking spending and 63; unencumbered homeowners and pension contributions 33
saving budget 61; *see also* budget/budgeting
self-invested personal pension (SIPP) 121, 144
selling, property 143
serviced accommodation, property 140–141
shorter-term repayment 76–78
shortfall or surplus, budget 63
short-term financial goals 54
short-term sacrifices 40–41; *see also* sacrifices, personal
single-pronged approach to pay off mortgage 49–51
SMART goal 56, 57; *see also* goal setting
social changes 114
socially acceptable savings goal 113
spare room, renting of 149
specific goal setting 55
spending 64, 65; estimate for budget 61; tracking 63; *see also* investments
state pension *119*
State Pension age (SPA) 114
statutory sick pay (SSP) 96–97
stress: due to debts 2, 15; family's well-being 91; financial 2, 17–20, *18*; housing 31; poor sleep quality 19, 28; psychological 2, 20; reducing by monthly mortgage payments 37
stress-sleep cycle 19, *20*

**T**

tax, mortgage overpayment and 123
term tracker mortgages 71

time-bound goal setting 55
tracker-rate mortgages 71; advantages
    of 74; compared with variable rate
    mortgages 72; disadvantages of 74
tracking progress 57
trade-off: considerations between
    investing and paying off mortgage
    106–107; overpayment and topping
    up pension 122–125
trading up, avoiding of 79
two-pronged approach to paying off
    mortgage 49–51
types of mortgages 70–74


U

uncertainties in life 87–90


V

variable budget 63; see also budget/
    budgeting

variable rate mortgage 71–73; advantages
    of 74; barriers 72–73; disadvantages
    of 74
vision board 55, 56
visual goal setting 55–57; see also goal
    setting


W

wealth protection 85–98; low savings
    in UK 95–96; mortgage payment
    protection insurance (MPPI) 95;
    mortgage success 86–87; protecting
    mortgage from risks of ill health
    91–95; by protection of property
    97–98; through life insurance
    90–91; through risk-reduction
    techniques 86–87; uncertainties
    in life and 87–90; welfare benefits
    96–97
welfare benefits 96–97
whole of life policy 90
wise money handling 161–162

Printed and bound by CPI Group (UK) Ltd, Croydon, CR0 4YY

02/10/2024

01040116-0018